Examples to Accompany
Descriptive Cataloging of Rare Books

Prepared by the
Bibliographic Standards Committee
of the
Rare Books and Manuscripts Section
(ACRL/ALA)

Association of College and Research Libraries
Chicago

Published by the Association of College and Research Libraries
A Division of the American Library Association
50 East Huron Street
Chicago, IL 60611-7295

ASSOCIATION OF

COLLEGE

& RESEARCH

LIBRARIES

ISBN: 0-8389-7672-7

This publication is printed on recycled paper.

Printed in the United State of America.

INTRODUCTION

Purpose and Audience

   Examples to Accompany Descriptive Cataloging of Rare Books is exactly what its title implies: a companion to *Descriptive Cataloging of Rare Books*, 2nd ed., Washington, D.C., Cataloging Distribution Service, Library of Congress, 1991 (*DCRB*). It is meant as an illustrative aid to catalogers and others interested in or needing to interpret rare book cataloging. As such, it is to be used in conjunction with the rules it illustrates, both in *DCRB* and in *AACR2*, and in the context of local institutional practice.

   Examples are particularly useful in rare book cataloging because of the complexity of many rare books and their corresponding catalog records. The variations in printing practices, lack of standardized title pages in early works, range of languages, and the artifactual aspects of rare books can all pose problems for the cataloger. Through use of examples, these potentially difficult areas can be clarified. In addition, the necessity of incorporating into rare book cataloging elements of other disciplines, such as descriptive bibliography, can be made easier for the cataloger by consulting examples as well as the appropriate manuals.

   This publication is aimed at all who catalog rare books according to *DCRB*. It will be especially useful to the novice rare book cataloger and to the cataloger who catalogs rare books infrequently. We hope that it will also be an aid to experienced rare book catalogers who are confronted with unfamiliar bibliographical problems or materials out of their usual areas of expertise. Others who may find this handbook helpful are those who seek to interpret rare book cataloging, including special collections reference librarians and researchers. We expect that it will also serve the needs of educators and trainers of rare book catalogers, in library schools, workshops and on-the-job training.

   The examples in this handbook are illustrative and not prescriptive. They are meant as models rather than standards, and should never be seen as substitutes for the rules from which they are derived. Catalogers will need to use judgment in adopting or adapting these examples for use in their work. They will want to consider the needs of the users of their collections in the contexts of both local cataloging policy and national standards. Still, we hope that this publication will promote effective and consistent use of rare book cataloging standards by providing models which illustrate those standards.

Background

   Examples to Accompany Descriptive Cataloging of Rare Books replaces the ten examples found on p. [55]-60 of *Bibliographic Description of Rare Books* (*BDRB*), the first edition of the rare book cataloging rules now known as *Descriptive Cataloging of Rare Books*. When *BDRB* was revised in 1990-91 by members of the Bibliographic Standards Committee of the Rare Books and Manuscripts Section of the Association of College and Research Libraries and staff members from the Library of Congress, examples were omitted from the resulting publication, in large part due to time constraints. Surveys conducted during the revision of *BDRB* revealed that many catalogers wished for more, and more complete, examples. Since it was not possible to satisfy this need during the revision of the rules, the Bibliographic Standards Committee undertook a project to prepare a separate publication containing examples.

   Work on the *Examples* began almost immediately after the publication of *DCRB*. A subcommittee of the Bibliographic Standards Committee prepared drafts of the *Examples* for discussion and revision at American Library Association meetings in 1992 and 1993. These drafts were based initially on the handbook developed by Suzy Taraba and Stephen R. Young for the Rare Book Cataloging class they taught at Columbia University's Rare Book School during the summers of 1986-91, and on Eric Holzenberg's handbook used in rare book cataloging workshops in the Chicago area. Other examples were solicited, primarily from other members and friends of the Bibliographic Standards Committee, to fill in gaps. No open

INTRODUCTION

solicitation for examples was conducted because of the difficulty of revising examples without the books in hand.

Scope

The aim of this publication is to illustrate *DCRB*, with special emphasis on those rules that are unusually complex, those that differ from *AACR2* and those that differ from *BDRB*. In addition, the most important rule options in *DCRB* are illustrated, including double punctuation, graphic process and minimal-level cataloging. The examples encompass materials from a wide range of dates, places of publication and languages.

Reflecting the scope of the code it illustrates, *Examples to Accompany Descriptive Cataloging of Rare Books* covers only monographic and serials cataloging. Records illustrating "special collections cataloging" (as defined in *DCRB*, Appendix E: *DCRB* Code for Records, p. 77) are also not included among the *Examples*. In this context, "special collections cataloging" means fuller use of notes, access points, and other elements that are not specifically called for in *AACR2* or its predecessors, but that follow the spirit of *DCRB* without following its rules completely. The decision regarding when to use *DCRB*, "special collections cataloging," or *AACR2* is a matter of institutional policy. This handbook includes examples of fifteenth-through twentieth-century materials cataloged according to full *DCRB*.

Two options receive special treatment in this handbook. The double punctuation option is illustrated by cataloging the same item twice (Examples 26A and 26B), once using prescribed punctuation, and once using the option of double punctuation. In similar fashion, the catalog record used to illustrate minimal-level cataloging appears in three versions (Examples 40A, 40B and 40C), first as a full-level record, then as the briefest allowable minimal-level record, and finally as a minimal-level record with options applied. (See *DCRB*, Appendix D: Minimal-Level Records, p. 75-76.)

Arrangement and Format of Examples

The examples in the handbook are arranged chronologically by the date of publication of the item cataloged. This arrangement is supplemented by title, author, rule number and topical indexes.

Each example includes an illustration of the title page (or title page substitute) as well as the resulting catalog record(s). Some examples also include other relevant illustrations, such as the colophon or a text sample used to determine proper transcription of early letter forms. For ease of use, the illustration for each example is on the page facing the corresponding catalog record. The cataloger can thus open the handbook to a two-page spread for convenient study of the title page and record.

MARC-coded records are used in recognition of the fact that most catalogers are now preparing catalog records for an online database rather than a manual card catalog. Each catalog record is a "generic" USMARC record with full tagging for record-level variable fields. The form of tagging used in the records is neither OCLC- nor RLIN-based, nor does it reflect the specific practice of any of the other major utilities or local online catalogs. However, labels such as "Contents:" and "References:" which are generally system-supplied in an automated environment do not appear in the examples. Fixed fields are omitted, as are any variable fields which occur before the main entry. (See *DCRB*, Appendix E: *DCRB* Code for Records, p. 77, for proper coding of MARC field 040.)

Because conventions for tagging copy-specific information vary so widely among the major bibliographic utilities and online systems, most copy-specific fields in the examples are not numerically coded but are labeled with mnemonic tags used only in this publication. These tags are **LN** (for "Local Note"), **LAE** (for "Local Added Name Entry") and **LTE** (for "Local

iv

INTRODUCTION

Added Title Entry"). In addition, all copy-specific fields (including those 755 fields which provide access to copy-specific aspects of the item cataloged) are highlighted by a vertical slash to the left of the field tag. In recording copy-specific information, catalogers should follow the requirements of their bibliographic utilities and their local online catalogs. The note area of the catalog record will vary considerably from institution to institution, in terms of both coding and wording. Nevertheless, the treatment of copy-specific information found in these examples may be used as a model to inform local policy.

Conventions of modern punctuation are generally used in the examples. (See *DCRB* 0E, par. 5, p. 4.) Appropriate modern punctuation is, to some extent, a matter of cataloger's judgment. The *Examples* follow *AACR2* prescribed punctuation, as well as some conventions that are used in *AACR2* but are not specifically prescribed, such as the practice of inserting commas before and after the word "or" (or its equivalent) that often signals an alternative title.

Since subject practice is not covered in descriptive cataloging codes such as *DCRB* and *AACR2*, and it is essentially the same for rare books as it is for other materials, the Committee decided that subject headings could be omitted from the examples without diminishing the usefulness of the publication. This decision was supported by a variety of other factors, including space considerations. Similarly, some, but not all, other access points are used in the examples. Those access points which are present include title tracings called for in *DCRB* Appendix A: Title Access Points (p. 67-68), thesaurus terms (655 and 755 fields) from the thesaurus publications prepared by the Bibliographic Standards Committee (see bibliography), and some special tracings which might typically be used in a special collections library (printer, former owner, etc.). The cataloger's use of all of these access points will depend on local policy; thus, there has been no attempt to use all possible title tracings, thesaurus terms, or special tracings for any given record. Hierarchical Place Name Access (MARC field 752) is not used in the examples.

Below each catalog record are listed the principal *DCRB* rules used in its creation. Although the most significant rules associated with each example are listed, it is impossible to cite in the available space every rule used by the cataloger of any given item. Some of the most basic rules (such as those governing transcription of early letter-forms) apply to virtually every situation encountered in rare book cataloging; these rules have been listed only where there are particularly clear examples of their use. However, the topical index will in most cases list every occurrence of such a rule, whether or not it has been cited in the rule list for a particular example. In all cases, when a rule includes an option, the primary rule (rather than the option) is illustrated unless specifically stated otherwise.

The list of rules in each example includes both the rule number and a brief phrase which describes the topic of the rule and/or specific points or options which are illustrated. Reference numbers to the left of the listed rules allow the cataloger to identify exactly where in each record a given rule is illustrated. These reference numbers correspond to the reference numbers found to the left of many of the fields in each catalog record. The cataloger can work both from the catalog record to see which rules were followed in any part of that record and from the list of rules to see an illustration of the application of that rule.

Catalog records found in the *Examples* will necessarily vary from the records for the same items which appear in the national utilities or in local institutional catalogs. The records in the utilities and local catalogs have not been routinely updated to reflect the change in cataloging codes. In preparing this handbook, example records were edited for clarity, consistency and accuracy.

The *Examples* are drawn from real cataloging prepared by several rare book catalogers at a variety of institutions. Experienced catalogers realize that there is frequently more than one acceptable or appropriate way to solve a cataloging problem. Local policy may influence the way in which some rules are applied, individual interpretation of some rules can vary, and of course each cataloger brings different experience and judgment to the job. The Committee

INTRODUCTION

believes that the variety inherent in these examples accurately reflects the realities of rare book cataloging. By showing more than one solution to a given problem, we hope that the *Examples* will be more helpful to catalogers than would a strictly uniform approach to similar situations.

Corrections and Suggestions

Corrections, suggestions and questions about *Examples to Accompany Descriptive Cataloging of Rare Books* should be directed to the RBMS Bibliographic Standards Committee. Any correspondence regarding this publication should be addressed to

Chair, Bibliographic Standards Committee
Rare Books and Manuscripts Section
ACRL/ALA
50 East Huron Street
Chicago IL 60611

Attention: Handbook of Examples

Acknowledgments

This handbook was prepared by the Bibliographic Standards Committee of the Rare Books and Manuscripts Section of the Association of College and Research Libraries. The subcommittee charged with preparing draft documents was chaired first by Suzy Taraba and later by Eric Holzenberg. Other members of the subcommittee were Elizabeth Herman, Nixie Miller, Eve Pasternak, and Jocelyn Sheppard. Other members of the Bibliographic Standards Committee during the work on this publication were Laura Stalker (Chair), Virginia Bartow, Jain Fletcher, Elizabeth Johnson, Rita Lunnon, Deborah Ryszka, Joe Springer, and Belinda Urquiza.

Many catalogers prepared the records on which this publication is based. The cataloging of examples from Duke University was done by Nixie Miller, Dan Rettberg, Diane Shaw and Suzy Taraba; from Loyola University by Eric Holzenberg; from Yale University by Cynthia Crooker, James Fox and Stephen R. Young; from the Lilly Library by Steve Cape, Diane Bauerle and Elizabeth Johnson; from the Folger Shakespeare Library by Henry Raine; from the Library Company of Philadelphia by Deborah J. Leslie. Librarians who contributed extensive comments include Elizabeth Herman (Getty Center), Brian Hillyard (National Library of Scotland), Elizabeth Johnson (Lilly Library), George Mulally (University of Iowa), Eve Pasternak (Pierpont Morgan Library), Alan Poor (University of Chicago), Henry Raine (Folger Shakespeare Library), Patrick Russell (University of California, Berkeley) and Joe Springer (Goshen College). The topical index of the *Examples* is based on that prepared by David Rich (John Carter Brown Library) for *DCRB*.

Significant institutional support for this project was given by Duke University and Loyola University. In addition, many people in Perkins Library at Duke University provided invaluable assistance and technical support, including Dan Daily, Cheryl Gates, Sandra Hack Polaski, Glenda LaCoste, Greg Lyon, Diane Sutton, Cheryl Thomas and Nelda Webb.

The Committee extends sincere thanks to all who helped make this project possible.

PHOTOGRAPHY CREDITS

RARE BOOK CATALOGING TOOLS

Cataloging Rules

Anglo-American Cataloguing Rules, Second Edition. 1988 Revision. Chicago: American Library Association, 1988.

CONSER Editing Guide. Prepared by the staff of the Serial Record Division under the direction of the CONSER Operations Coordinator. Washington, D.C.: Serial Record Division, Library of Congress, 1986 (and updates)

Descriptive Cataloging of Rare Books, Second Edition. Washington, D.C.: Cataloging Distribution Service, Library of Congress, 1991.

ISBD(A): International Standard Bibliographic Description for Older Monographic Publications (Antiquarian). 2nd rev. ed. München; New York: Saur, 1991.

Thesauri, &c.

Binding Terms: A Thesaurus for Use in Rare Book and Special Collections Cataloguing. Prepared by the Bibliographic Standards Committee of the Rare Books and Manuscript Section. Chicago: Association of College and Research Libraries, 1988.

Carter, John. ABC for Book-Collectors. 6th ed., with corrections & additions by Nicolas Barker. New Castle, Del.: Oak Knoll Books, 1992.

Genre Terms: A Thesaurus for Use in Rare Book and Special Collections Cataloguing. 2nd ed. Prepared by the Bibliographic Standards Committee of the Rare Books and Manuscript Section. Chicago: Association of College and Research Libraries, 1991.

Paper Terms: A Thesaurus for Use in Rare Book and Special Collections Cataloguing. Prepared by the Bibliographic Standards Committee of the Rare Books and Manuscript Section. Chicago: Association of College and Research Libraries, 1990.

Printing and Publishing Evidence: Thesauri for Use in Rare Book and Special Collections Cataloguing. Prepared by the Standards Committee of the Rare Books and Manuscript Section. Chicago: Association of College and Research Libraries, 1986.

Provenance Evidence: Thesaurus for Use in Rare Book and Special Collections Cataloguing. Prepared by the Standards Committee of the Rare Books and Manuscript Section. Chicago: Association of College and Research Libraries, 1988.

"Relator Terms for Rare Book, Manuscript, and Special Collections Cataloguing." Prepared by the Standards Committee of the Rare Books and Manuscript Section. 3rd ed. College & Research Libraries News, v. 48, no. 9 (Oct. 1987), p. 553-557. [Supplemented by correction note on p. 645, v. 48, no. 10 (Nov. 1987)]

Type Evidence: A Thesaurus for Use in Rare Book and Special Collections Cataloguing. Prepared by the Bibliographic Standards Committee of the Rare Books and Manuscript Section. Chicago: Association of College and Research Libraries, 1990.

CATALOGING TOOLS

VanWingen, Peter M. and Stephen Paul Davis. Standard Citation Forms for Published Bibliographies and Catalogs Used in Rare Book Cataloging. Washington: Library of Congress, 1982. And supplement: "Citation Forms for Bibliographies Appearing in Journals or as Component Parts of Larger Works." Prepared by the Standards Committee of the Rare Books and Manuscript Section. College & Research Libraries News, v. 49, no. 8 (Sept. 1988), p. 525-526.

Descriptive Bibliography

Bowers, Fredson T. Principles of Bibliographical Description. Princeton: Princeton University Press, 1949. [1986 reprint: Winchester, U.K.: St. Paul's Bibliographies]

Fingerprints = Empreintes = Impronte. Paris: Institut de Recherche et d'Histoire des Textes, 1984. Supplemented by: Nouvelles des empreintes = Fingerprint Newsletter (no. 1- 1981- Paris: Institut de Recherche et d'Histoire des Textes)

Gaskell, Philip. A New Introduction to Bibliography. Oxford: Clarendon Press, 1974 (c1972). "Reprinted with corrections."

McKerrow, R. B. An Introduction to Bibliography for Literary Students. Oxford: Oxford University Press, 1965 (c1927)

McKerrow, R. B. "Some Notes on the Letters I, J, U and V in Sixteenth-Century Printing." The Library, 3rd series, no. 1 (1910)

Modern Forms of Latin Place Names

Grässe, Johann Georg Theodor. Orbis Latinus: Lexicon Lateinischer Geographischer Namen des Mittelalters und der Neuzeit. Grossausgabe, bearb. und hrsg. von Helmut Plechl unter Mitarbeit von Sophie-Charlotte Plechl. Braunschweig: Klinkhardt & Biermann, 1972.

Peddie, R. A. Place Names in Imprints: An Index to the Latin and Other Forms Used on Title Pages. London: Grafton & Co., 1932. [1968 reprint: Detroit: Gale Research Co.]

Abbreviations and Contractions Used in Early Printing

Cappelli, Adriano. Lexicon Abbreviaturarum = Dizionario di Abbreviature Latine ed Italiane Usate nelle Carte e Codici Specialmente del Medio-Evo ... 4. ed. Milano: Hoepli, 1949.

Cappelli, Adriano. The Elements of Abbreviation in Medieval Latin Paleography. Translated by David Heimann and Richard Kay. Lawrence, Kansas: University of Kansas Libraries, 1982. [translation of Cappelli's introduction to the Lexicon Abbreviaturarum]

Chronology

The Book of Calendars. Frank Parise, editor. New York: Facts on File, 1982.

Cappelli, Adriano. Cronologia, Cronografia e Calendario Perpetuo, dal Principio dell'Era Cristiana ai Nostri Giorni. 3. ed. aggiornata ed ampliata. Milano: Hoepli, 1969.

CATALOGING TOOLS

Pseudonyms and Anonyms

Barbier, A. A. Dictionnaire des Ouvrages Anonymes. 3e éd., rev. et augm. Paris: P. Daffis, 1872-1879. [1964 reprint: Paris: G. P. Maisonneuve & Larose]

Halkett, Samuel and John Laing. Dictionary of Anonymous and Pseudonymous English Literature. 3rd rev. and enl. ed., John Horden, editor. Harlow: Longman, 1980-

Holzmann, Michael and Hanns Bohatta. Deutsches Anonymen-Lexicon, 1501-1850. Weimar: Gesellschaft der Bibliophilen, 1902. [Reprints: Hildesheim: Olms, 1961; New York: Olms, 1984]

Melzi, Gaetano. Dizionario di Opere Anonime e Pseudonime di Scrittori Italiani, o Como Che sia Aventi Relazione all'Italia. Milano: L. di Giacomo Pirola, 1848-1859. [1960 reprint: New York: Burt Franklin]

Quérard, Joseph-Marie. Les Supercheries Littéraires Dévoilées. 2. éd., considérablement augm., publiée par Gustave Brunet et Pierre Janet. Paris: P. Daffis, 1869-1870. [1960 reprint: Hildesheim: G. Olms]

False and Fictitious Imprints

Brunet, Gustave. Imprimeurs Imaginaires et Libraires Supposés. Paris: Tross, 1866. [1963 reprint: New York: Burt Franklin]

Parenti, Marino. Dizionario dei Luoghi di Stampa Falsi, Inventati o Suppositi in Opere di Autori e Traduttori Italiani. Firenze: Sansoni, 1951.

Weller, Emil Ottokar. Die Falschen und Fingierten Druckorte. 2. verm. und verb. Aufl. Leipzig: W. Engelmann, 1864. [1970 reprint: Hildesheim: Olms]

Woodfield, Denis B. Surreptitious Printing in England, 1550-1640. New York: Bibliographical Society of America, 1973.

Incunabula

British Museum. Dept. of Printed Books. Catalogue of Books Printed in the XVth Century Now in the British Museum. London: Printed by order of the Trustees, 1908-1971.

Copinger, Walter Arthur. Supplement to Hain's Repertorium Bibliographicum. Berlin: J. Altmann, 1926. [1950 reprint: Milano: Görlich]

Gesamtkatalog der Wiegendrucke. Herausgegeben von der Kommission für den Gesamtkatalog der Wiegendrucke. Leipzig: K. W. Hiersemann, 1925- [Reprint: Stuttgart: A. Hiersemann; New York: H.P. Krauss, 1968-]

Goff, Frederick R. Incunabula in American Libraries: A Third Census of Fifteenth-Century Books Recorded in North American Collections. New York: Bibliographical Society of America, 1964. [1973 reprint: Millwood, N.Y.: Kraus Reprint Co.]

CATALOGING TOOLS

Hain, Ludwig Friedrich Theodor. Repertorium Bibliographicum, in quo Libri Omnes ab Arte Typographica Inventa Usque ad Annum MD. Typis Expressi, Ordine Alphabetico vel Simpliciter Enumeratur vel Adcuratus Recensiter. Stuttgart: J. G. Cotta, etc., 1826-1838. [1948 reprint: Milano: Görlich]

Incunable Short Title Catalogue. [Available through the RLIN or BLAISE databases]

Indice Generale degli Incunaboli delle Biblioteche d'Italia. A cura del Centro Nazionale d'Informazioni Bibliografiche. Roma: Libreria dello Stato, 1943-1981.

Panzer, Georg Wolfgang Franz. Annales Typographici ab Artis Inventae Origine ad Annum MD. Nuremburg: J. B. Zeh, 1793-1803.

Polain, Louis. Catalogues des Livres Imprimés au Quinzième Siècle des Bibliothèques de Belgique. Bruxelles: Pour la Société des Bibliophiles & Iconophiles de Belgique, 1932.

Proctor, Robert. An Index to the Early Printed Books in the British Museum. London: K. Paul, 1898-1903.

General Bibliographies

British Museum. Dept. of Printed Books. General Catalogue of Printed Books to 1955. Photolithographic Edition. London: Trustees of the British Museum, 1959-1966.

Brunet, Jacques Charles. Manuel du Libraire et de l'Amateur de Livres. 5 éd., originale entièrement refondue et augm. d'un tiers par l'auteur ... Paris: Firmin Didot frères, fils et cie, 1860-1865 (and: Supplément. Par MM. P. Deschamps et G. Brunet, 1878-1880)

Grässe, Johann Georg Theodor. Trésor de livres rares et précieux. Berlin: J. Altmann, 1922.

Index Aureliensis: Catalogus Librorum Sedecimo Saeculo Impressorum. Editio princeps. Aureliae Aquensis, 1962-

National Union Catalog, Pre-1956 Imprints: A Cumulative Author List Representing Library of Congress Printed Cards and Titles Reported by Other American Libraries. London: Mansell, 1968-1980. (and Supplement, 1980-1981)

Bibliothèque Nationale (France). Départment des Imprimés. Catalogue Générale des Livres Imprimés de la Bibliothèque Nationale: Auteurs. Paris: Impr. Nationale, 1897-

National Bibliographies

The Americas

Evans, Charles. American Bibliography: A Chronological Dictionary of All Books, Pamphlets, and Periodical Publications Printed in the United States of America From the Genesis of Printing in 1639 Down to and Including the Year 1820. Chicago: Privately printed for the author by the Blakely Press, 1903-1959. [reprints: New York: P. Smith, 1941-1959; Metuchen, N.J.: Mini-Print Corp., 1967]

CATALOGING TOOLS

Medina, José Toribio. Biblioteca Hispano-Americana (1493-1810). Santiago de Chile, 1898-1907. [1968 reprint: Amsterdam: L. Israel]

Sabin, Joseph. A Dictionary of Books Relating to America, from its Discovery to the Present Time. New York, 1868-1936. [Reprints: New York: Mini-Print Corp., 196-?; Metuchen, N.J.: Scarecrow Press, 1966]

Thompson, Lawrence Sidney. The New Sabin: Books Described by Joseph Sabin and his Successors, Now Described Again on the Basis of Examination of Originals, and Fully Indexed by Title, Subject, Joint Authors, and Institutions and Agencies. Troy, N.Y.: Whitston Pub. Co., 1974-

Belgium & Netherlands

British Library. Catalogue of Books from the Low Countries 1601-1621 in the British Library. Compiled by Anna E. C. Simoni. London: British Library, 1990.

British Museum. Dept. of Printed Books. Short-Title Catalogue of Books Printed in the Netherlands and Belgium and of Dutch and Flemish Books Printed in Other Countries from 1470 to 1600 Now in the British Museum. London: Trustees of the British Museum, 1965.

France

Baudrier, Henri Louis. Bibliographie Lyonnaise: Recherches sur les Imprimeurs, Libraires, Relieurs et Fondeurs de Lettres de Lyon au XVIe Siècle. Publiées et continuées par J. Baudrier. Lyon: Librairie Ancienne d'Auguste Brun, 1895-1921.

British Museum. Dept. of Printed Books. Short-Title Catalogue of Books Printed in France and of French Books Printed in Other Countries from 1470 to 1600 Now in the British Museum. London: Trustees of the British Museum, 1924 (and supplements)

Cioranescu, Alexandre. Bibliographie de la Littérature Française du Seizième Siècle. Collaboration et préface de V.-L. Saulnier. Paris: C. Klincksieck, 1959.

Cioranescu, Alexandre. Bibliographie de la Littérature Française du Dix-septième Siècle. Paris: Editions du Centre National de la Recherche Scientifique, 1965-1966.

Cioranescu, Alexandre. Bibliographie de la Littérature Française du Dix-huitième Siècle. Paris: Editions du Centre National de la Recherche Scientifique, 1969.

Goldsmith, Valentine Fernande. A Short-Title Catalogue of French Books, 1601-1700, in the Library of the British Museum. Folkestone: Dawsons, 1969-1973.

Germany

British Museum. Dept. of Printed Books. Short-Title Catalogue of Books Printed in the German-Speaking Countries and German Books Printed in Other Countries from 1455-1600 Now in the British Museum. London: Trustees of the British Museum, 1962.

CATALOGING TOOLS

Verzeichnis der im Deutschen Sprachbereich Erschienenen Drucke des XVI. Jahrhunderts: VD 16. Stuttgart: Hiersemann, 1983-

Great Britain

British Library. The Eighteenth Century Short Title Catalog. [available on microfiche, CD ROM, or through the RLIN or BLAISE databases]

Pollard, William and G. R. Redgrave. A Short-Title Catalogue of Books Printed in England, Scotland, Ireland, and of English Books Printed Abroad, 1475-1640. 2nd ed. London: Bibliographical Society, 1976-1991.

Wing, Donald Goddard. Short-Title Catalogue of Books Printed in England, Scotland, Ireland, Wales, and British America and of English Books Printed in Other Countries, 1641-1700. 2nd ed., rev. & enl. New York: Index Committee of the Modern Language Association, 1972-

Italy

British Library. Catalogue of Seventeenth Century Italian Books in the British Library. London: The Library, 1986.

British Museum. Dept. of Printed Books. Short-Title Catalogue of Books Printed in Italy and of Italian Books Printed in Other Countries from 1465 to 1600 Now in the British Museum. London: Trustees of the British Museum, 1958.

Le Edizioni Italiane del XVI Secolo: Censimento Nazionale. Roma: Istituto Centrale per il Catalogo Unico delle Biblioteche Italiane e per le Informazioni Bibliografiche, 1985-

Spain & Portugal

British Library. Catalogue of Books Printed in Spain and of Spanish Books Printed Elsewhere in Europe Before 1601 Now in the British Library. 2nd ed. London: British Library, 1989.

British Museum. Dept. of Printed Books. Short-Title Catalogues of Spanish, Spanish-American and Portuguese Books Printed Before 1601 Now in the British Museum. By H. Thomas. London: British Museum, 1966.

Palau y Dulcet, Antonio. Manual del Librero Hispano-Americano: Bibliografía General Española e Hispano-Americana desde la Invención de la Imprenta Hasta Nuestros Tiempos, con el Valor Comercial de los Impresos Descritos. 2. ed. corr. y aumentada por el autor. Barcelona: A. Palau, 1948-1977.

Silva, Innocencio Francisco da. Diccionário Bibliographico Portuguez. Lisboa: Na Imprensa Nacional, 1858-1923. [1972 reprint]

EXAMPLES

A.

B.

B-526
(B460)
Biblia latina. [Mainz: Printer of the 42-line Bible (Johann Gutenberg and Peter Schoeffer?), about 1454-55, not after Aug. 1456.] f°. 42 ll.

C.

B-607
(B541)
— (cum glossa ordinaria Walafridi Strabonis aliorumque et interlineari Anselmi Laudunensis). [Strassburg: Adolf Rusch, for Anton Koberger, not after 1480.] f°.
N.B: Apparently printed with types borrowed from Johann Amerbach — cf BMC I 92 or GW 4282.

EXAMPLE 1: A. First page of text (image reduced 55 percent) B-C. Goff entries B-526 and B-607 (source of supplied title)

EXAMPLE 1

CATALOG RECORD

ref. no.

	130 0	Bible. $l Latin. $s Vulgate. $f not after 1480.
1	245 10	[Biblia Latina : $b cum glossa ordinaria Walafridi Strabonis aliorumque et interlineari Anselmi Laudunensis]
2,3,4,5,6,7	260	[Strasbourg? : $b Adolf Rusch?, for Anton Koberger?, $c not after 1480]
	300	4 v. ; $c 48 cm. (fol.)
8	500	Title from Goff.
9	500	Commonly thought to have been printed by Rusch with types borrowed from Johann Amerbach. Some authorities write that Amerbach printed this edition himself at Basel.
10	500	Printed in two columns of interlineated text surrounded by a glossary.
10	500	Press figures.
11	510 4	BM 15th cent., $c I, 92
11	510 4	Copinger, W.A. Incunabula Biblica, $c 44
11	510 4	Goff $c B-607
11	510 4	GW $c 4282
11	510 4	Hain-Copinger $c 3173
11	510 4	Polain $c 682A
11	510 4	Proctor $c 299
12	LN	Rubricated initials in red, blue and green.
12	LN	Library has v. 1 and 4; both vols. bound in blind-stamped half calf, paste paper over wooden boards, metal and leather clasps.
12	LN	Ms. note: Iste liber est canonicorum regularum monasterij Beat[a]e Virginis in [illegible].
	700 00	Walahfrid Strabo, $d 807?-849.
	700 00	Anselmus, $c of Laon, $d d. 1117.
	700 10	Rusch, Adolf, $d fl. 1466-1489, $e printer.
	700 10	Koberger, Anton, $d ca. 1440-1513, $e bookseller.
	700 10	Amerbach, Johannes, $d 1441?-1513, $e printer.
	755	Press figures (Printing) $2 rbpri
	755	Clasps (Binding) $2 rbbin
	755	Wooden boards (Binding) $2 rbbin
	755	Paste papers (Paper) $2 rbpap

PRINCIPAL *DCRB* RULES ILLUSTRATED

ref. no.

1	0C3	(no title page; title supplied from reference source)
2	4A2	(publication information based on several reference sources)
3	4B1	(supplied place of publication given in English form)
4	4B12	(probable place of publication supplied from reference source)
5	4C1	(publisher statement includes printer)
6	4C8	(probable publisher supplied from reference source)
7	4D6	(date uncertain; "terminal date" pattern used)
8	7C3	(source of title proper note)
9	7C8	(publication note)
10	7C10	(physical description note)
11	7C14	(references to published descriptions; required for incunabula)
12	7C18	(copy-specific note)

Α . Β . Γ . Δ . Ε . Ζ . Η . Θ . Ι . Κ . Λ . Μ . Ν . Ξ . Ο . Π . Ρ . Σ . Τ . Υ . Φ . Χ . Ψ . Ω .

ΑΙ . ΑΎ . ΕΙ . ΕΎ . ΟΙ . ΟΎ .   Αἰ . Ηἰ . Ωἰ . Υἰ .

ΝΘΟΛΟΓΊΑ ΔΙΑΦΌΡΩΝ ἘΠΙΓΡΑΜΜΆΤΩΝ, ἈΡΧΑΊΟΙΣ ΣΥΝ
ΤΕΘΕΙΜΈΝΩΝ ΣΟΦΟῖΣ, ἘΠΙ ΔΙΑΦΌΡΟΙΣ ῪΠΟΘΈΣΕΣΙΝ, ἙΡΜΗ
ΝΕΊΑΣ ἘΧΌΝΤΩΝ ἘΠΊΔΕΙΞΙΝ . ΚΑῚ ΠΡΑΓΜΆΤΩΝ Ἢ ΓΕΝΟΜΈ
ΝΩΝ, Ἢ ῺΣ ΓΕΝΟΜΈΝΩΝ ἈΦΉΓΗΣΙΝ . ΔΙΗΡΗΜΈΝΟΥ ΔΕῚΣ Ἐ
ΠΤΆ ΤΜΉΜΑΤΑ ΤΟῦ ΒΙΒΛΊΟΥ ΚΑῚ ΤΟΎΤΩΝ ῈΙΣ ΚΕΦΆΛΑΙΑ
ΚΑΤΆ ΣΤΟΙΧΕῖΟΝ ΔΙΕΚΤΕΘΕΙΜΈΝΩΝ, ΤΆΔΕ ΠΕΡΙΈΧΕΙ ΤῸ
ΠΡῶΤΟΝ . ΕΙΣ ΑΓῶΝΑΣ . ΕΙΣ ἌΜΠΕΛΟΝ . ΕΙΣ ἈΝΑΘΉΜΑ
ΤΑ . ΕΙΣ ἈΝΑΓΉΡΟΥΣ . ΑΝΔΡΕΊΟΥΣ . ΑΝΤΑΠΌΔΟΣΙΝ . ΑΠΕΙ
ΛῊΝ . ΑΡΕΤῊΝ . ΑΣΕΒΕῖΣ . ΑΣΌΤΟΥΣ . ΑΥΛΗΤᾺΣ . ΑΥΤΆΡ
ΚΕΙΑΝ . ΒΊΟΝ ἈΝΘΡΏΠΙΝΟΝ . ΒΡΈΦΗ . ΓΆΜΟΝ . ΓῆΡΑΣ .
ΓΡΑΜΜΑΤΙΚΟῪΣ . ΓΥΝΑῖΚΑΣ . ΔΈΝΔΡΑ . ΔΙΚΑΙΟΣΎΝΗΝ .
ΔΊΚΗΝ . ΔΥΣΤΥΧΊΑΝ . ΕΛΕΟΝ . ΕΛΠΊΔΑΣ . ΕΠΑΊΝΟΥΣ .
ΕΡΩΤΑ . ΕΥΣΈΒΕΙΑΝ . ΕΥΤΥΧΊΑΝ . ΕΥΧΑΡΊΣΤΟΥΣ . ΕΥΧῊΝ
ΕΧΘΡΟΎΣ . ΖῶΑ . ΖΩῊΝ . ΗΧῸ . ΘΆΛΑΣΣΑΝ . ΘΆΝΑΤΟΝ .
ΘΕΟῪΣ . ΙΑΤΡΟῪΣ . ΙΧΘΎΑΣ .   ΚΆΛΛΟΣ . ΚΌΛΑΚΑΣ . ΚΡΙ
ΤΆΣ . ΛΟΓΟΓΡΑΦΊΑΝ . ΜΑΙΝΟΜΈΝΟΥΣ . ΜΑΘΉΜΑΤΑ . ΜΈ
ΘΗΝ . ΜΕΤΡΙΌΤΗΤΑ . ΜῖΣΟΣ . ΜΗΤΡΥΙᾺΝ . ΝΝΉΜΗΝ .
ΜΥΣΤΉΡΙΟΝ . ΜΈΜΨΙΝ . ΝΑΟῪΣ . ΝΑΥΆΓΙΟΝ . ΝΑΥΤΙ
ΛΊΑΝ . ΝῆΑΣ . ΝΉΣΟΥΣ . ΟῖΝΟΝ . ΟΡΝΙΣ . ΠΑΙΔΙᾺΝ .
ΠΑΝΟΎΡΓΟΥΣ . ΠΑΡΑΜΥΘΊΑΝ . ΠΑΤΡΊΔΑ . ΠΗΓῊΝ . ΠΛΟΥ
ΤΟῦΝΤΑΣ . ΠΟΙΗΤᾺΣ . ΠΟΙΜΈΝΑΣ . ΠΌΛΕΜΟΝ . ΠΌΛΕΙΣ .
ΠΟΝΗΡΟΎΣ . ΠΌΡΝΑΣ . ΠΟΤΑΜΟῪΣ . ΠΤΩΧΟῪΣ . ΣΙΩΠῊΝ .
ΣΟΦΊΑΝ . ΣΎΓΚΡΙΣΙΝ . ΣΩΦΡΟΣΎΝΗΝ . ΤΙΜῊΝ . ΤΎΧΗΝ .
ΥΠΕΡΟΨΊΑΝ . ΦΉΜΗΝ . ΦΙΛΑΡΓΎΡΟΥΣ . ΦΙΛΊΑΝ . ΦΙΛΟΣΌΦΟΥΣ .
ΦΙΛΟΣΤΟΡΓΊΑΝ . ΦΡΌΝΗΣΙΝ . ΦΡΟΝΤΊΔΑΣ . ΧΡΌΝΟΝ . ὩΡΆΣ .

B.

IMPRESSVM FLORENTIAE PER LAVRENTIVM FRANCISCI
DI ALOPA VENETVM . III . IDVS AVGVSTI . M . CCCC
LXXXXIIII . Χ

EXAMPLE 2: A. First page of text B. Colophon

EXAMPLE 2

CATALOG RECORD

ref. no.

	130 0	Greek anthology.
1,2	245 10	Anthologia diaphor⁻on epigrammat⁻ōn / $c archaiois syntetheimen⁻on sophois ...
3,4,5,6,7,8,9	260	Impressum Florentiae : $b Per Laurentium Francisci de Alopa Venetum, $c III. idus Augusti [11 Aug.] 1494.
10,11	300	[560] p. ; $c 22 cm. (4to)
12	500	Title taken from opening words of text, leaf A1v, transliterated.
13,14	500	First edition; compiled by Planudes; edited by Janus Lascaris.
15	500	Imprint from colophon.
15	500	At head of first leaf: Greek alphabet and diphthongs.
16	500	Signatures (Greek alphabet): [Alpha]-2[Kappa]^8 chi^8(chi8 blank).
17	500	Space for initial letter of first word of title left blank by printer; spaces for initials throughout.
18	510 4	GW $c 2048
18	510 4	BM 15th cent., $c VI, p. 666
18	510 4	Hain $c 1145
18	510 4	Goff $c A765
18	510 4	Pellechet $c 802
19	LN	Library's copy lacks terminal blank.
19	LN	With the bookplate of the Broxburne library on back endpaper; front endpapers with the bookplate of William Charles de Meuron, Earl Fitzwilliam, and a modern bookplate "pro viribus summis contendo, ex libris A.E."
19	LN	Bound by P. Bozerain le jeune in black straight grain morocco, gilt flower and leaf borders and spine, edges gilt; spine skilfully repaired.
	700 10	Laurentius, Venetus, $e printer.
	700 10	Lascaris, Janus, $d 1445?-1535, $e ed.
	700 10	Planudes, Maximus, $d ca. 1260-ca. 1310, $e comp.
	LAE	Bozerain, $c le jeune, $e binder.

PRINCIPAL *DCRB* RULES ILLUSTRATED

ref. no.

1	0G	(missing guide letter supplied in transcription)
2	1B5	(title taken from opening words of text)
3	4A2	(imprint from colophon)
4	4B1	(place of publication transcribed as it appears)
5	4B2	(words or phrases associated with place name transcribed)
6	4C2	(words or phrases preceding publisher statement transcribed)
7	4D1	(day and month in date transcribed)
8	4D2, par. 1	(roman numerals in date transcribed as arabic numerals)
9	4D2, par. 5	(Roman-style date)
10	5B8	(pages not numbered)
11	5D1, par. 3	(format)
12	7C3	(source of title proper note)
13	7C6 (1)	(authorship note)
14	7C7	(edition and bibliographic history note)
15	7C8	(publication note)
16	7C9	(signatures note; gatherings signed with unavailable characters)
17	7C10	(physical description note)
18	7C14	(references to published descriptions; required for incunabula)
19	7C18	(copy-specific note)

A.

C Tractatus de sensu composito ꝗ diuiso
magistri Gulielmi hētisberi. Cū
expositione infrascripto
ruꝫ ꞉ videlicet.

C Magistri Alexandri Sermonete.
C Magistri Bernardini Petri de lā
ducijs.
C Magistri Pauli pergulensis.
C Magistri Baptiste de fabriano.

B.

C Impressum Uenetijs p̄ Jacobum
Pentium de Leuco. Anno domini
M.cccccj. Die.xvij. Julij regnante
Augustino Barbadico serenissimo
Uenetiarum Principe.

EXAMPLE 3: **A.** Title page **B.** Colophon to vol. 1, showing usage of i/j and u/v

EXAMPLE 3

CATALOG RECORD

ref. no.

	100 1	Heytesbury, William, $d fl. 1340.
	240 10	De sensu composito et diviso
2,3,4,5	245 10	Tractatus de sensu composito [et] diuiso Magistri Gulielmi He[n]tisberi : $b cu[m] expositione infrascriptoru[m] videlicet, Magistri Alexandri Sermonete, Magistri Bernardini Petri de La[n]ducijs, Magistri Pauli Pergulensis, Magistri Baptiste de Fabriano.
1,2,6,7, 8,9,10,11	260	Impressum Venetijs : $b P[er] Iacobum Pentium de Leuco, $c anno Domini 1501 die xvij. Iulij.
12,13	300	23, [1], 24, 18 leaves ; $c 21 cm. (4to)
14	500	Each part has separate colophon, some with printer's device.
14	500	Imprint from colophon to pt. 1.
14	500	Colophons have dates: pt. 1, Die xvij. Iulij, 1501; pt. 2, Die xx. Nouembris, 1500; pt. 3, Die iij. Decembris, 1500.
15	500	Signatures: A-C^8, ^{2}A-C^8 a^8 b^{10}.
16	500	Black letter type; text printed in double columns.
17	510 4	BM STC Italian, $c p. 322
18	| LN	With: Pergola, Paolo della, d. 1455. [Compendium logicae] Logica Magistri Pauli Pergulensis. Impressum Venetijs : Per Io. Baptistam Sessa, anno salutis 1501 vltimo Kal's Decembris [1 Dec.]
	700 10	Sermoneta, Alexander.
	700 10	Landucius, Bernardinus Petrus.
	700 10	Pergola, Paolo della, $d d. 1455.
	700 10	Fabriano, Baptista de.
19	740 01	Tractatus de sensu composito et diviso Magistri Gulielmi Hentisberi.
20	740 01	De sensu composito et diviso.

PRINCIPAL *DCRB* RULES ILLUSTRATED

ref. no.

1	0H, par. 5	(gothic capitals J and U treated as I and V)
2	0J2	(contractions and abbreviations expanded to full form)
3	1B1	(statement of responsibility inseparably linked to title proper)
4	1D5	(other title information with inseparable statements of responsibility)
5	1G7	(titles of address in statements of responsibility)
6	4A2	(imprint from colophon)
7	4B2	(words or phrases associated with place name transcribed)
8	4C2	(words or phrases preceding publisher transcribed)
9	4D1	(day, month, words and phrase in date transcribed)
10	4D2, par. 1	(roman numerals in date transcribed as arabic numerals)
11	4D8	(additional dates given in note)
12	5B1, par. 1	(leaves printed on both sides, numbered on one side)
13	5D1, par. 3	(format)
14	7C8	(publication note)
15	7C9	(signatures note)
16	7C10	(physical description note)
17	7C14	(references to published descriptions)
18	7C19	(copy-specific "with:" note)
19	App. A.0J2	(added entry for title proper with expansion of contractions)
20	App. A.1B1	(added entry for chief title)

A.

Omnis q̃ a ratione suscipit de aliqua re institutio a diffinitione profiscisci
debet ut intelligatur id de quo disputetur

dialektos ratu est disputatio
dialerete differet est fode dialetur

Logica magistri Pau
li pergulensis.

C Impressum Uenetijs per Jo. Bapti
stam Sessa . Anno salutis.1501.vltimo
Kal's Decembris.

B.

EXAMPLE 4: A. Title page B. Colophon, showing usage of i/j and u/v

EXAMPLE 4

CATALOG RECORD

ref. no.

	100	1	Pergola, Paolo della, $d d. 1455.
	240	10	Compendium logicae
2,3	245	10	Logica Magistri Pauli Pergulensis.
1,4,5,6,7,8	260		Impressum Venetijs : $b Per Io. Baptistam Sessa, $c anno salutis 1501 vltimo Kal's Decembris [1 Dec.]
9,10,11	300		[72] p. ; $b ill. (woodcuts) ; $c 21 cm. (4to)
12	500		Imprint from colophon.
13	500		Signatures: a-i⁴.
14	500		Printer's devices on t.p. and colophon; initials.
14	500		Text in black letter type.
15	510	4	EDIT 16 $c B704
16	LN		With: Heytesbury, William, fl. 1340. [De sensu composito et diviso] Tractatus de sensu composito [et] diuiso Magistri Gulielmi He[n]tisberi ... Impressum Venetijs : P[er] Iacobum Pentium de Leuco, anno Domini 1501 die .xvij. Iulij.

PRINCIPAL *DCRB* RULES ILLUSTRATED

ref. no.

1	0H, par. 5	(gothic capitals J and U treated as I and V)
2	1B1	(statement of responsibility inseparably linked to title proper)
3	1G7	(title of address in statement of responsibility)
4	4A2	(imprint from colophon)
5	4B2	(words or phrases associated with place name transcribed)
6	4C2	(words or phrases preceding publisher statement transcribed)
7	4D1	(day, month, words and phrases in date transcribed)
8	4D2, par. 5	(Roman-style date)
9	5B8	(pages not numbered)
10	5C1	(illustrations; **option:** describe graphic process or technique)
11	5D1, par. 3	(format)
12	7C8	(publication note)
13	7C9	(signatures note)
14	7C10	(physical description note)
15	7C14	(references to published descriptions)
16	7C19	(copy-specific "with:" note)

Or
tho
gra
phia
Clariſſimi
Oratoris
Ga
ſpa
rini
Ber
go
menſis
De uerbis quibus frequentior uſus eſt
 et in quibus ſepius a recta ſcribédi via
deceditur: et tam de compoſitis q̃ ſim/
plicibus penes ordinem litterarum: ne
quis in querédo falli poſſit: ac de dipḥ
tongis et ratione punctandi.

EXAMPLE 5: Title page

EXAMPLE 5

CATALOG RECORD

ref. no.

	100 1	Barzizza, Gasparino, $d ca. 1360-1431.
	240 10	Orthographia
1,2,3	245 10	Orthographia clarissimi oratoris Gasparini Bergomensis : $b de uerbis quibus frequentior usus est [et] in quibus sepius a recta scribe[n]di via deceditur ...
4,5,6,7	260	[Venice : $b s.n., $c 151-?]
8,9	300	[160] p. ; $c 22 cm. (4to)
10	500	Signatures: a^8 b-t^4.
11	500	Woodcut initials (used by de Luere, Venice, 1511, 1514).
12	510 4	Index Aureliensis, $c 114.329
12	510 4	EDIT 16 $c B704
13	LN	From the library of Paez, with signature.
	LAE	Paez, $e former owner.
	755	Autographs (Provenance) $2 rbprov

PRINCIPAL *DCRB* RULES ILLUSTRATED

ref. no.

1	0J2	(contractions and abbreviations expanded to full form)
2	1B1	(statement of responsibility inseparably linked to title proper)
3	1B7	(lengthy title abridged)
4	4A2	(elements of publication, etc. area supplied from several reference sources)
5	4B10	(place of publication supplied from reference source)
6	4C9	(publisher unknown)
7	4D6	(date uncertain; "probable decade" pattern used)
8	5B8	(pages not numbered)
9	5D1, par. 3	(format)
10	7C9	(signatures note)
11	7C10	(physical description note)
12	7C14	(references to published descriptions)
13	7C18	(copy-specific note)

A.

Súma

Angelica : ve

nerabilis in xpo patris
fratris. angeli de clauasio : ordi
nis minox de obseruantia :
cum quibusdam nouis z
oppoxtunis additioni
bus eiusdem : quisqᷓ
suo Congruo loco miro ordi
ne situatis. nuper cum gra
tia ē priuilegio illu
strisimi dominii
consilii rogato
rum prout
in eo.

B.

Ad lectorem.

Dumio angelicas gētēᷓ andif loꝗas
Dic cupis : p̄sens plege lege lector op̄
Dic sacros canōes. Dic z duilia īra.
Dic sancte inuepīēs religionis opes.
Maxia mstoꝗ ꝗ vix dabat añ libroꝛ
, Sarciꝗ. id ągeli. dat tibi súma breuis
Augel'e auctor : sacri dec̄ ordis igēs
Seraphici : e tāīe Religīois honos.
Sj plūbo veneta foꝛmat paga. i vrbe
Dul²cui p̄m̄° nūc daf artis honos
Brixia cui pfia est claroꝛ tecta viroꝛ
Dro quo tota viget nobilitata dom̄
Auctore atᷓ opus ip̄ressuᷓ felicia dōa
Clauassina mia terra beata viro
Nec carlera min̄°gēs felix vñ creatus.
Augel° ągelicis dign²adesse choris

℮ Explicit súma angelica de casib°cō
scie p̄fratrē Angelū de clauasio ꝯpilla
ta niaxia cū dilig ̄itia reuisa z ̄hdeli
studio emēdata : sicut ipsum opus p se
satis attestabif. Uenetijs ip̄reisa per
Alexandrum de paganinis. anno dūl.
M. cccc xl die. viij. mia reij.

EXAMPLE 6: A. Title page B. Colophon, showing usage of i/j and u/v

EXAMPLE 6

CATALOG RECORD

ref. no.

	100 0	Angelo Carletti, $d 1411-1495.
1,3,4,5,6	245 10	Su[m]ma angelica venerabilis in [Christo] Patris Fratris Angeli de Clauasio Ordinis Mino[rum] de Obseruantia : $b cum quibusdam nouis [et] opportunis additionibus eiusdem, quisq[ue] suo congruo loco miro ordine situatis.
1,2,3,7,8,9,10	260	Venetiis : $b I[m]pressa per Alexandrum de Paganinis, $c anno D[omi]ni 1511, die viij. Marcij.
11	300	[18], 458 leaves ; $c 19 cm. (8vo)
12	500	Imprint from colophon.
13	500	Signatures: pi^8 a^{10}, ^{2}a^{16} b-z^{16} [et]^{16} [con]^{16} [rum]^{16} A-B^{16} c^{10}
14	500	Text in double columns, 48 lines to a full column.
14	500	Title in red.
15	| LN	Library's copy in old calf-backed oak boards, with clasp; annotated throughout in an old hand.
16	740 01	Summa angelica venerabilis in Christo Patris Fratris Angeli de Clavasio Ordinis Minorum de Observantia.
17	740 01	Suma angelica venerabilis in xpo Patris Fratris Angeli de Clauasio Ordinis Mino. de Obseruantia.
	| 755	Annotations (Provenance) $2 rbprov
	| 755	Wooden boards (Binding) $2 rbbin

PRINCIPAL *DCRB* RULES ILLUSTRATED

ref. no.

1	0H, par. 3	(convert to uppercase or lowercase according to AACR2; transcribe i/j and u/v according to pattern in main text)
2	0H, par. 5	(gothic capitals J and U treated as I and V)
3	0J2	(contractions and abbreviations expanded to full form)
4	1A2, par. 3	(privilege statement omitted without using mark of omission)
5	1B1	(statement of responsibility inseparably linked to title proper)
6	1D2, par. 1	(other titles or phrases following title proper treated as other title information)
7	4A2	(imprint from colophon)
8	4C2	(words or phrases preceding publisher statement transcribed)
9	4D1	(day, month, words and phrase in date transcribed)
10	4D2, par. 1	(roman numerals in date transcribed as arabic numerals)
11	5D1, par. 3	(format)
12	7C8	(publication note)
13	7C9	(signatures note; gatherings signed with unavailable characters)
14	7C10	(physical description note)
15	7C18	(copy-specific note)
16	App. A.0J2	(added entry for title proper with expansion of contractions)
17	App. A.0J2	(**option:** added entry for title proper without expansion of contractions)

A.

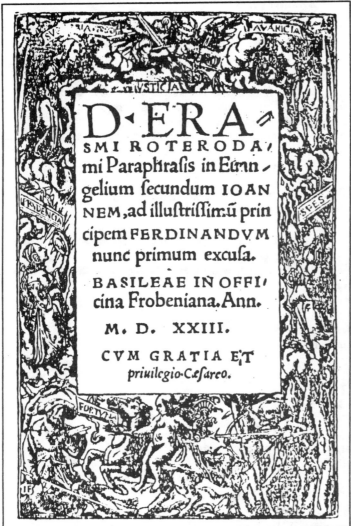

D·ERA
SMI ROTERODA,
mi Paraphrafis in Euan,
gelium fecundum IOAN
NEM, ad illuftriffim.ū prin
cipem FERDINANDVM
nunc primum excufa.

BASILEAE IN OFFI,
cina Frobeniana. Ann.

M. D. XXIII.

CVM GRATIA ET
priuilegio·Cæfareo.

BASILEAE IN AEDIBVS IOANNIS
FROBENII, MENSE APRILI.
AN. M. D. XXIII.

B.

C.

IN EVANGE. IOAN. PARAP.   ERASMI ROT. CAP.   1
prophetici dignitatē angelus dictus eſt,tamē nihil ali   non ipſa lux. Chriſtus igitur pro temporis diſpenſa,
ud erat quàm homo, plurimis quidē dei donis largi,   tione abuſus eſt errore ludæorū,& autoritate ioan,

EXAMPLE 7: **A.** Title page **B.** Colophon **C.** Running title

EXAMPLE 7

CATALOG RECORD

ref. no.

	100 1	Erasmus, Desiderius, $d d. 1536.
	240 10	Paraphrasis in Evangelium secundum Joannem
1,2,3,4,5	245 10	D. Erasmi Roterodami Paraphrasis in Euangelium secundum Ioannem / $c ad illustrissimu[m] principem Ferdinandum nunc primum excusa.
6,7	260	Basileae : $b In Officina Frobeniana, $c ann. 1523.
8,9	300	[400] p. ; $c 17 cm. (8vo)
10	500	Running title: In Euang. Ioan. Paraph. Erasmi Rot.
11	500	Colophon: Basileae in aedibus Ioannis Frobenij, mense Aprili. An. M.D.XXIII.
12	500	Signatures: a-z^8 A-B^8.
13	500	Title within historiated metalcut border by Jakob Faber after Holbein. Cf. Hollstein, F.W.H. German engravings, etchings and woodcuts, v. 14A, no. 40.
13	500	Decorative borders; initials; side-notes; printer's device on last leaf.
13	500	Italic type.
14	500	"Illustrissimo Principi, D. Ferdinando ... Erasmus Roterodamus S.D.": p. [3]-[20].
14	500	"Erasmus Rot. Pio Lectori S.D.": p. [395]-[399].
15	LN	Bound in contemporary blind-stamped pigskin over boards, clasps lacking.
	700 10	Faber, Jakob, $d fl. 1520, $e engraver.
	700 10	Froben, Johann, $d 1460-1527, $e printer.
	700 10	Holbein, Hans, $d 1497-1543, $e ill.
16	740 01	Paraphrasis in Euangelium secundum Joannem.
17	740 01	Paraphrasis in Evangelium secundum Ioannem.
18	740 01	In Euang. Ioan. Paraph. Erasmi Rot.
	755	Headlines (Printing) $2 rbpri
	755	Printers' devices (Printing) $2 rbpri
	755	Borders (Type evidence) $2 rbtyp
	755	Pigskin bindings (Binding) $y 16th century. $2 rbbin
	755	Blind tooled bindings (Binding) $y 16th century. $2 rbbin

PRINCIPAL *DCRB* RULES ILLUSTRATED

ref. no.

1	0H, par. 3	(convert to uppercase or lowercase according to AACR2; transcribe i/j and u/v according to pattern in main text)
2	0J2	(contractions and abbreviations expanded to full form)
3	1A2, par. 3	(privilege statement omitted without using mark of omission)
4	1B1	(statement of responsibility inseparably linked to title proper)
5	1G12	(statement of responsibility without explicitly named person or body)
6	4D1	(phrase in date transcribed)
7	4D2, par. 1	(roman numerals in date transcribed as arabic numerals)
8	5B8	(pages not numbered)
9	5D1, par. 3	(format)
10	7C4	(variation in title note)
11	7C8	(publication note)
12	7C9	(signatures note)
13	7C10	(physical description note)
14	7C16	(informal contents note)
15	7C18	(copy-specific note)
16	App. A.0H	(added entry for title proper in modern orthography)
17	App. A.1B1	(added entry for chief title)
18	App. A.7C4-5	(added entry for title variant)

A.

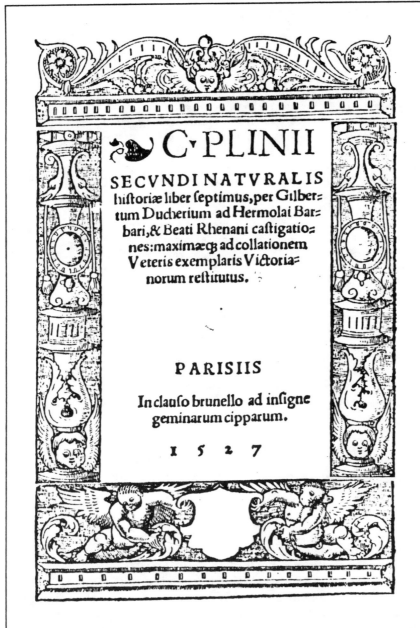

C·PLINII
SECVNDI NATVRALIS
hiſtoriæ liber ſeptimus, per Gilber=
tum Ducherium ad Hermolai Bar=
bari,& Beati Rhenani caſtigatio=
nes: maximæcɜ ad collationem
Veteris exemplaris Victoria=
norum reſtitutus.

PARISIIS

In clauſo brunello ad inſigne
geminarum cipparum.

1 5 2 7

.VII.

talem ſolem
eſtimandum

. Fol.ij.facie
ras quidem:
n morſu non
rcule.Fol.iiij
e.ij.melius le
olio.vij.facie
ſecūda.Editis geminis raram.& paulopoſt in læ=
ua fœminas.

PARISIIS
Apud Prigentium Caluarin.

B.

EXAMPLE 8: A. Title page B. Colophon

EXAMPLE 8

CATALOG RECORD

ref. no.

	100 0	Pliny, $c the Elder.
	240 10	Naturalis historia. $n Liber 7
1,2,3,4	245 10	C. Plinii Secundi Naturalis historiae liber septimus / $c per Gilbertum Ducherium ad Hermolai Barbari, & Beati Rhenani castigationes maximaeq[ue] ad collationem veteris exemplaris Victorianorum restitutus.
2,4,5	260	Parisiis : $b [Apud Prigentium Caluarin] in clauso Brunello ad insigne Geminarum Cipparum, $c 1527.
6,7,8	300	xxxv leaves ; $c 17 cm. (8vo)
9	500	Publisher's name from colophon: Parisiis Apud Prigentium Caluarin.
10	500	Signatures: a-d^8 e^4(-e4).
11	510 4	BN $c CXXXIX, column 94
	700 10	Ducher, Gilbert, $d d. ca. 1538.
	700 10	Barbaro, Ermolao, $d 1454-1493.
	700 10	Rhenanus, Beatus, $d 1485-1547.
12	740 01	Naturalis historiae liber septimus.

PRINCIPAL *DCRB* RULES ILLUSTRATED

ref. no.

1	0H, par. 2	(transcribe Latin ligature as component letters)
2	0H, par. 3	(convert to uppercase or lowercase according to AACR2; transcribe i/j and u/v according to pattern in main text)
3	0J2	(contractions and abbreviations expanded to full form)
4	1B1	(statement of responsibility inseparably linked to title proper)
5	4C4	(publisher's address on t.p. in lieu of name; publisher's name supplied)
6	5B1, par. 1	(leaves printed on both sides, numbered on one side)
7	5B1, par. 2	(leaves numbered in roman numerals, transcribed lowercase as they appear)
8	5D1, par. 3	(format)
9	7C8	(publication note)
10	7C9	(signatures note)
11	7C14	(references to published descriptions)
12	App. A.1B1	(added entry for chief title)

¶Magna
Carta in F.
wherunto is added
more statutz than e=
uer was imprynted
in any one boke be=
fore this tyme/ with
an Almanacke & a
Calender to
know the
mootes.
Necessarye for all
yong studentes of
the lawe.

ANNO Domini M.
CCCCC.XXXIX

¶Here en
deth Magna Carta
with diuers other
Statutes. Impryn=
ted at Lond in F ...
strete/by me Ro=
bert Redman
dwellynge
at the sy
gne of
the George/nexte to
saynt Dunstones
Churche.

✠

Anno dñi, M. ccccc.
xxxix.

EXAMPLE 9: A. Title page B. Colophon

EXAMPLE 9

CATALOG RECORD

ref. no.

	110 1	England.
	240 10	Laws, etc. (Antiqua statuta)
1,2	245 10	Magna carta in F : $b wherunto is added more statut[es] than euer was imprynted in any one boke before this tyme : with an alminacke [and] a calender to know the mootes : necessarye for all yong studiers of the lawe.
1,3,4,5,6,7,8	260	Imprynted at Lond[on] in Fletestrete : $b By me Robert Redman ..., $c anno Domini 1529 [i.e. 1539]
9,10	300	[8], 148, [4], 74, [3] leaves ; $c 14 cm. (12mo)
11	500	Contains Magna carta, and statutes passed prior to the reign of Edward III.
12	500	Text in Latin and Law French.
13	500	In two parts; pt. 1, originally published by R. Pynson in 1508, here has the same few additions as Redman's 1525 edition (STC 9269); Redman added the second part in 1532 (STC 9271).
14	500	Place of publication and name of printer from colophon, which gives 1539 as the date of printing.
15	500	Signatures: pi^8 A-T^{12} v^2.
16	500	Title, almanac (leaves pi1v-pi8v) and colophon in red and black; initials.
16	500	Black letter type.
16	500	Errors in foliation: leaves 101, 110-119 numbered 1001, 1010-1019; 108 repeated.
17	510 4	STC (2nd ed.) $c 9273
18	LN	Library's copy in old boards; stamps and label of St. Ignatius College; signature on flyleaf of N. Blagdon, and date 1813.
	655 7	Legal works $z England $y 16th century. $2 rbgenr
	LAE	Blagdon, N., $e former owner.
	LAE	St. Ignatius College (Chicago, Ill.), $e former owner.
	730 02	Magna Carta. $f 1539.
	755	Black letter types (Type evidence) $z England $y 16th century. $2 rbtyp

PRINCIPAL *DCRB* RULES ILLUSTRATED

ref. no.

1	0J2	(contractions and abbreviations expanded to full form)
2	1D2, par. 1	(other titles or phrases following title proper treated as other title information)
3	4A2	(place of publication and and printer statement from colophon)
4	4B2	(words or phrases associated with place name transcribed)
5	4C2	(words or phrases preceding publisher statement transcribed)
6	4D1	(phrase in date transcribed)
7	4D2, par. 1	(roman numerals in date transcribed as arabic numerals)
8	4D2, par. 4	(incorrect date transcribed as it appears; corrected date added)
9	5B1, par. 1	(leaves printed on both sides, numbered on one side)
10	5B3	(foliation sequence includes unnumbered leaves)
11	7C1	(nature, scope or artistic form note)
12	7C2	(language of publication note)
13	7C7	(edition and bibliographic history note)
14	7C8	(publication note)
15	7C9	(signatures note)
16	7C10	(physical description note)
17	7C14	(references to published descriptions)
18	7C18	(copy-specific note)

ספר מתורגמן

מעשה ידי אמן · בביאור כל מלות · חמודות
גם קלות · הנמצאות בלשון ארמי · בתרגום
אונקלוס ויונתן וירושלמי · והשיב
את כל אשר דבר י · בטרט
אליה המחבר ·

משם מה בעיר איזנא · על ידי שלמה בן אם · עם עמר קוס
הסרחא בלשון חמו סרחילגיס כתוב וחתוס מיד חרטים
החיבר את כלא היה עם ארס סרעיסהא תוך
ועתך עמר עמס · מהיס תם ת
סא יחיה לחתס רב בלא
עשרם

ף

א.

ברוך א עליון אשר נתן כח לעבדו בן אמתו להחל
ולכלות ספר הזה · · · · וכן יהי רצון מלפניו
שיחיה עמי לחדדס שאר הספרים
כאשר בלבבי

ותהי השלמתו בעיר איזנא שבת חמשת
אלפים ושלש מאות ואחת
לבריאת עולם

כל אילן טוב עשא פרי טוב

ב.

EXAMPLE 10: A. Title page B. Colophon
(images reduced 55 percent)

EXAMPLE 10

CATALOG RECORD

ref. no.

	100 1	Levita, Elijah, $d 1468 or 9-1549.
	240 10	Meturgeman
	245 10	Sefer Meturgeman : $b ma'a´seh yede oman : be-ve'ur kol milot, .hamurot gam .kalot, ha-nimtsa'ot be-lashon arami be-Targum On.kelos .ve-Yonatan .ve-Yerushalmi / $c .ve-he.tiv et kol asher diber bi-ferat Eliyah ha-me.haver.
1,2,3,4,5	260	Nidpas poh ba-'ir Iznah [Isny, Germany] : $b 'Al yede Pa.vilu´s Vagiu´s ..., $c meha-yom yom 1, 21 yamim le-.hodesh Av 301 [14 Aug. 1541] li-ferat.
6,7,8	300	[4], 164, [2] leaves ; $c 29 cm. (fol.)
9	500	Hebrew and Aramaic.
10	500	Colophon: Barukh E. 'Elyon asher natan koa.h le-avdo ben amato le-he.hel ule-khalot sefer ha-zeh ve-khen yehi ratson mi-lefana.v she-yihyeh 'imi le-hadpis shear ha-sefarim ka-asher be-levavi .va-tehi ha-shelemato ba-'ir Iznah shenat .hamishat alafim .ve-shalosh me'ot .ve-a.hat li-vri'at 'olam.
10	500	Colophon has printer's device with initials P.V. in Hebrew characters and motto: Kol ilan .tov no´se peri .tov.
11	500	Signatures: pi^4 1-27^6 28^4.
12	500	Gatherings signed in both Hebrew characters and Arabic numerals.
12	500	Leaves numbered in Hebrew characters.
13	LN	From the library of the Yeshivat Magen Avraham, with the yeshivah's name and shelfmark stamped in gold on the spine.
13	LN	Imperfect copy: T.p. lacking, supplied in facsimile.
	700 10	Fagius, Paulus, $d 1504-1549, $e printer.
	LAE	Yeshivat Magen Avraham, $e former owner.
	755	Printers' devices (Printing) $2 rbpri
	755	Printers' mottoes (Printing) $2 rbpri
	755	Non-Latin characters (Type evidence) $x Hebrew $y 16th century. $2 rbtyp
	755	Shelf marks (Provenance) $2 rbprov

PRINCIPAL *DCRB* RULES ILLUSTRATED

ref. no.

1	4B2	(words or phrases associated with place name transcribed)
2	4B3	(modern form of place name added)
3	4C2	(words or phrases preceding publisher statement transcribed)
4	4D1	(day, month, words and phrase in date transcribed)
5	4D2, par. 5	(non-Christian-era date)
6	5B1, par. 1	(leaves printed on both sides, numbered on one side)
7	5B3	(foliation sequence includes unnumbered leaves)
8	5D1, par. 3	(format)
9	7C2	(language of publication note)
10	7C8	(publication note)
11	7C9	(signatures note)
12	7C10	(physical description note)
13	7C18	(copy-specific note)

A.

LA PRIMA PARTE
DELLE HISTORIE DEL
SVO TEMPO
DI MONS. PAOLO
GIOVIO VESCOVO
DI NOCERA,

*Tradotte per M. Lodoui-
co Domenichi.*

IN VINEGIA appreſſ
M D L
S. BAR

LA
SECONDA PARTE
DELL'HISTORIE DEL
SVO TEMPO
DI MONS. PAOLO
GIOVIO VESCOVO
DI NOCERA,

*Tradotte per M. Lodoui-
co Domenichi.*

CON LA TAVOLA DELLE COSE NO-
TABILI, NOVAMENTE AGGIVNTA.

IN VINEGIA appreſſo Bartholomeo Ceſano.
M D L I I I I.

S. BARTOLO

B.

EXAMPLE 11: A. Title page to vol. 1 B. Title page to vol. 2

EXAMPLE 11

CATALOG RECORD

ref. no.

	100 1	Giovio, Paolo, $d 1483-1552.
	240 10	Historiae sui temporis. $l Italian
1,2	245 13	La prima[-seconda] parte delle Historie del suo tempo / $c di Mons. Paolo Giouio vescouo di Nocera ; tradotte per M. Lodouico Domenichi.
1,3,4,5	260	In Vinegia : $b Appresso Bartholomeo Cesano, $c 1553-1554.
6,7	300	2 v. ; $c 16 cm. (8vo)
8	500	Translation of: Historiae sui temporis.
9	500	Vol. 2 has title: La seconda parte dell'Historie del suo tempo ... ; con la tauola delle cose notabili, nouamente aggiunta.
10	500	Title vignettes (printer's device); initials.
10	500	Vol. 1: 526 [i.e. 534], [2] leaves (the last 2 leaves blank); v. 2: 398, [26] leaves.
10	500	Error in paging: v. 1, leaves 529-534 numbered 521-526.
11	| LN	Library's copy in old vellum-backed boards; book labels of Louis Thompson Rowe; stamp "S. Bartolo" on t.p.
	700 10	Domenichi, Lodovico, $d 1515-1564, $e tr.
	700 10	Cesano, Bartholomeo, $e printer.
	| LAE	Rowe, Louis Thompson, $e former owner.
12	740 01	Historie del suo tempo.
13	740 01	Prima parte delle historie del suo tempo.
13	740 01	Seconda parte dell'historie del suo tempo.
	755	Printers' devices (Printing) $z Italy $y 16th century. $2 rbpri
	| 755	Bookplates (Provenance) $2 rbprov
	| 755	Stamps (Provenance) $2 rbprov

PRINCIPAL *DCRB* RULES ILLUSTRATED

ref. no.

1	0H, par. 3	(convert to uppercase or lowercase according to AACR2; transcribe i/j and u/v according to pattern in main text)
2	1B4	(volume designations transcribed as part of title proper)
3	4B2	(words or phrases associated with place name transcribed)
4	4C2	(words or phrases preceding publisher statement transcribed)
5	4D2, par. 1	(roman numerals in date transcribed as arabic numerals)
6	5B20	(**option:** pagination of individual volumes given in note)
7	5D1, par. 3	(format)
8	7C2	(language of publication note; translation)
9	7C4	(variation in title note)
10	7C10	(physical description note)
11	7C18	(copy-specific note)
12	App. A.1B1	(added entry for chief title)
12	App. A.7C4-5	(added entry for other title)

EXAMPLE 12: Title page

EXAMPLE 12

CATALOG RECORD

ref. no.

	100 1	Valla, Lorenzo, $d 1406-1457.
	240 10	Elegantiae
1,2,3,4	245 10	Laurentij Vallae Elegantiarum Latinae linguae libri sex ; eiusdem De reciprocatione sui, & suus, libellus.
2,5,6	250	Ad veterum denu`o codicum fidem / $b ab Ioanne Raenerio emendata omnia.
2,7	260	Lugduni : $b Apud haered. Seb. Gryphij, $c 1561.
8,9	300	754, [54] p. ; $c 13 cm. (16mo)
10	500	Signatures: a-z^8 A-2D^8 2E^4.
11	500	Text in italic type.
11	500	Printer's device on t.p., with motto: Virtute duce, comite fortuna.
11	500	Leaves 2E3 and 2E4 blank.
12	510 4	Baudrier, H.L. Bib. lyonnaise, $c VIII, p. 302
12	510 4	Adams $c V184
13	504	Includes bibliographical references and index.
14	LN	Imperfect copy: worm holes through p. 643-664 (leaves S2-T4), affecting text.
14	LN	Contemporary full vellum binding, gilt-tooled red morocco spine label, all edges gilt.
	700 10	Raenerius, Joannes, $d 16th cent.
	700 12	Valla, Lorenzo, $d 1406-1457. $t De reciprocatione sui et suus libellus. $f 1561.
18	740 01	De reciprocatione sui, & suus, libellus.
16,18	740 01	De reciprocatione sui, et suus, libellus.
17	740 01	Elegantiarum Latinae linguae libri sex.
15	740 01	Lavrentii Vallae Elegantiarvm Latinae libri sex.
	755	Vellum bindings (Binding) $2 rbbin
	755	Gilt edges (Binding) $2 rbbin
	755	Printers' devices (Printing) $2 rbpri
	755	Printers' mottoes (Printing) $2 rbpri
	755	Italic types (Type evidence) $y 16th century. $2 rbtyp

PRINCIPAL *DCRB* RULES ILLUSTRATED

ref. no.

1	0H, par. 2	(transcribe Latin ligature as component letters)
2	0H, par. 3	(convert to uppercase or lowercase according to AACR2; transcribe i/j and u/v according to pattern in main text)
3	1B1	(statement of responsibility inseparably linked to title proper)
4	1E1	(two or more works by one author, without collective title)
5	2B1	(words or phrases associated with edition statement transcribed)
6	2C1	(statement of responsibility relating to edition)
7	4C2	(words or phrases preceding publisher statement transcribed)
8	5B3	(pagination sequence includes unnumbered pages)
9	5D1, par. 3	(format)
10	7C9	(signatures note)
11	7C10	(physical description note)
12	7C14	(references to published descriptions)
13	7C16	(informal contents note)
14	7C18	(copy-specific note)
15	App. A.0H	(added entry for title proper with letters transcribed as they appear)
16	App. A.0J2	(added entry for title with expansion of contractions)
17	App. A.1B1	(added entry for chief title)
18	App. A.1E1-2	(added entry for title of additional work)

HISTOIRE
DE TOVTES
CHOSES MEMORA-
BLES, TANT ECCLESIAS-
TIQVES QVE SECVLIERES,
Aduenues depuis soixante dix- huict ans en
toutes les parties du monde.

Composee premierement par Laurent Surius, & depuis
traduite en François, & continuee iusques au-
iourd'huy, Par IACQVES ESTOVR-
NEAV Sainctongeois.

Edition derniere.

A PARIS,
Chez Guillaume Chaudiere, ruë sainct Iaques,
à l'enseigne du Temps, & de
l'Homme sauuage.
M. D. LXXVIII.

AVEC PRIVILEGE DV ROY.

EXAMPLE 13: Title page

EXAMPLE 13

CATALOG RECORD

ref. no.

	100 1	Surius, Laurentius, $d 1522-1578.
	240 10	Commentarius brevis rerum in orbe gestarum ab anno salutis 1500 usque in annum 1568. $l French
1,2	245 10	Histoire de toutes choses memorables, tant ecclesiastiques que seculieres, aduenues depuis soixante dix-huict ans en toutes les parties du monde / $c composee premierement par Laurent Surius ; & depuis traduite en fran.cois, & continuee iusques auiourd'huy, par Iaques Estourneau sainctongeois.
	250	Edition derniere.
1,3,4,5	260	A Paris : $b Chez Guillaume Chaudiere ..., $c M.D.LXXVIII. [1578]
	300	[16], 468, [2] leaves ; $c 18 cm. (8vo)
6	500	Revised and updated translation of: Commentarius brevis rerum in orbe gestarum ab anno salutis 1500 usque in annum 1568.
7	500	Signatures: ˜a^8 ˜e^8 a-z^8 A-2M^8 2N^6.
8	500	Title vignette (publisher's device); initials; head-pieces.
9 |	LN	Library's copy in old limp vellum, with traces of ties; engraved armorial bookplate of Sir William Baird on t.p. verso; marginal notes in an old hand.
	700 10	Estourneau, Jacques.
|	LAE	Baird, William, $c Sir, $d b. 1654, $e former owner.
	755	Printers' devices (Printing) $z France $y 16th century. $2 rbpri
|	755	Armorial bookplates (Provenance) $z Scotland $y 17th century. $2 rbprov
|	755	Marginalia (Provenance) $2 rbprov

PRINCIPAL *DCRB* RULES ILLUSTRATED

ref. no.

1	0H, par. 1	(accents not added to "memorables," "ecclesiastique," etc.)
2	0H, par. 3	(convert to uppercase or lowercase according to AACR2; transcribe i/j and u/v according to pattern in main text)
3	4B2	(words or phrases associated with place name transcribed)
4	4C2	(words or phrases preceding publisher statement transcribed)
5	4D2, par. 1	(**option:** roman numerals in date transcribed; date in arabic numerals added)
6	7C2	(translation note)
7	7C9	(signatures note)
8	7C10	(physical description note)
9	7C18	(copy-specific note)

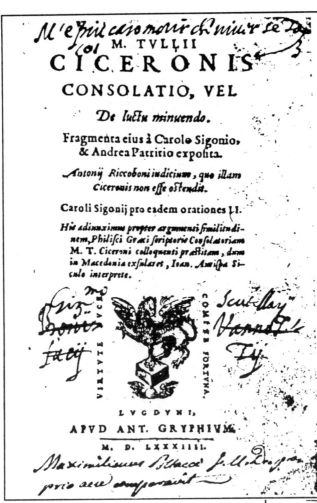

A.

per alios excudendos curauimus, so-
letes nobis, spero, erunt testes apud
neis, qui humanioris Musæ sensum
dò habebūt aliquem, tum noua hęc,
m te auspice & auctore, vir clarissi-
, primi nostratium damus, Tullianæ
olationis editio id testabitur:quam,
ianæ postremæ (ea ad manuscri-
:um fidem longè post omneis alias
garissima nobis sub prælo est)πἰϸιο-
ub rua nómine nunc emittimus. In
s enim apparere potiùs debeat, aut
is possit, quàm cuius illa beneficio
ostras manus primùm peruenit:qui-
que.ea sit illustris nominis apud omneis
auctoritate & gratia, vt commendare sine inuidia nouum opus, bonum aucto-
rem, simul visum, simul appetitum, pa-
trocinio suo tueri valeat ? Vix intimo
enim Adriatici emersus sinu, longis &
difficilibus itineribus Alpes transmise-
rat;domi tuæ, táquam in communi Mu-
sarum metato hospitio, cùm ei statim,
in publicum te manuducente progresso,
status quæstio à ciuibus nostris moueri
est cœpta : idque variis adeò dissentien-
tium doctorum iudiciis, vt non leuis
nunc nuper rumor,quanquam is incerto
auctore, iam percrebuerit,non fortuna-

A 3   rum,

B.

EXAMPLE 14: A. Title page B. Page of text, showing usage of i/j and u/v

EXAMPLE 14

CATALOG RECORD

ref. no.

	100 1	Cicero, Marcus Tullius.
	240 10	Consolatio
1,2,3,4,5	245 10	M. Tullij Ciceronis Consolatio, vel, De luctu minuendo : $b fragmenta eius `a Carolo Sigonio, & Andrea Patritio exposita : Antonij Riccoboni iudicium, quo illam Ciceronis non esse ostendit : Caroli Sigonij pro eadem orationes II : his adiunximus propter argumenti similitudinem, Philisci Graeci scriptoris Consolatoriam M.T. Ciceroni colloquenti praestitam, dum in Macedonia exsularet, Ioan. Aurispa Siculo interprete.
1,6	260	Lugduni : $b Apud Ant. Gryphium, $c 1584.
7	300	304 p. ; $c 13 cm. (16mo)
8	500	Signatures: A-T^8.
9	500	Publisher's device on t.p., with motto: Virtute duce, comite fortuna.
9	500	Initials; head-pieces.
10	510 4	Baudrier, H.L. Bib. lyonnaise, $c VIII, p. 389-390
11	LN	Limp vellum binding, ties lacking.
	700 10	Gryphius, Antoine, $d d. 1599, $e printer.
	700 10	Sigonio, Carlo, $d 1524?-1584.
	700 10	Nidecki, Andrzey Patrycy, $d 1530-1587.
	700 10	Aurispa, Giovanni, $d ca. 1376-1459.
12	740 01	Consolatio, vel, De luctu minuendo.
13	740 01	De luctu minuendo.
	755	Vellum bindings (Binding) $2 rbbin
	755	Limp bindings (Binding) $2 rbbin

PRINCIPAL *DCRB* RULES ILLUSTRATED

ref. no.

1	0H, par. 3	(convert to uppercase or lowercase according to AACR2; transcribe i/j and u/v according to pattern in main text)
2	1B1	(statement of responsibility inseparably linked to title proper)
3	1B3	(title proper inclusive of alternative title)
4	1D2, par. 1	(other titles or phrases following title proper treated as other title information)
5	1D5	(other title information with inseparable statements of responsibility)
6	4D2, par. 1	(roman numerals in date transcribed as arabic numerals)
7	5D1, par. 3	(format)
8	7C9	(signatures note)
9	7C10	(physical description note)
10	7C14	(references to published descriptions)
11	7C18	(copy-specific note)
12	App. A.1B1	(added entry for chief title)
13	App. A.1B3	(added entry for alternative title)

I DISCORSI DI NICO-LO MACHIAVELLI, SO-PRA LA PRIMA DECA DI TITO LIVIO.

Con due Tauole, l'vna de capitoli, & l'altra delle cose prin-cipali : & con le stesse parole di Tito Liuio a luo-ghi loro, ridotte nella volgar Lingua.

Nouellamente emmendati , & con somma cura ristampati.

IN PALERMO
Appresso gli heredi d'Antoniello degli Antonielli a xxviij.di
Genaio. 1 5 8 4.

EXAMPLE 15: Title page

EXAMPLE 15

CATALOG RECORD

ref. no.

	100 1	Machiavelli, Niccol`o, $d 1469-1527.
1,2,3	245 12	I discorsi di Nicolo Machiauelli, sopra la prima deca di Tito Liuio : $b con due tauole, l'vna de capitoli, & l'altra delle cose principali : & con le stesse parole di Tito Liuio a luoghi loro, ridotte nella volgar lingua.
4	250	Nouellamente emmendati, & con somma cura ristampati.
5,6,7,8,9,10	260	In Palermo [i.e. London] : $b Appresso gli heredi d'Antoniello degli Antonielli [i.e. John Wolfe], $c a xxviij. di genaio 1584 [i.e. 1585]
11,12	300	[16], 200 leaves ; $c 16 cm. (8vo)
13	500	False place of publication and fictitious publisher; actually printed in London by John Wolfe. Cf. Woodfield.
14	500	Collation: 8vo: *^{8} A-2C^8 [$4 signed (+D5, G5; -*3, A4; A1 signed 'B1')]; 216 leaves, ff. [16], 1-80 [81] 82-92 [93] 94-200 (misprinting 48 as '38', 57 as '67', 59 as '69', 61 as '71', 63 as '73', 136 as '135', 171 as '71').
15	500	Title vignette (printer's device); initials.
16	510 4	Woodfield, D.B. Surreptitious printing in England, $c 34
16	510 4	STC (2nd ed.) $c 17159
	755	Fictitious imprints (Publishing) $z England $y 16th century. $2 rbpub
	755	False imprints (Publishing) $z England $y 16th century. $2 rbpub
	755	Printers' devices (Publishing) $z England $y 16th century. $2 rbpub

PRINCIPAL *DCRB* RULES ILLUSTRATED

ref. no.

1	0H, par. 3	(convert to uppercase or lowercase according to AACR2; transcribe i/j and u/v according to pattern in main text)
2	1A1, par. 4	(colon precedes each unit of other title information)
3	1B1	(statement of responsibility inseparably linked to title proper)
4	2B3	(phrase referring to impression treated as edition statement)
5	4B2	(words or phrases associated with place name transcribed)
6	4B9	(false place of publication)
7	4C2	(words or phrases preceding publisher statement transcribed)
8	4C5	(fictitious publisher)
9	4D1	(day, month, words and phrase in date transcribed)
10	4D2, par. 6	(old style [i.e. Julian calendar] date)
11	5B3	(foliation sequence includes unnumbered leaves)
12	5D1, par. 3	(format)
13	7C8	(publication note)
14	7C9	(signatures note; **option**: provide full collation)
15	7C10	(physical description note)
16	7C14	(references to published descriptions)

A.

ELIZABETHÆ,
ANGLIAE REGINAE
HÆRESIN. CALVINIANAM
PROPVGNANTIS, SÆVISSIMVM
in Catholicos fui regni Edictum, quod
in alios quóque Reipublicæ Chri-
ftianæ Principes, contume-
lias continet indi-
gniſſimas.

Promulgatum Londini 29.Nouembris. 1591.

Cum reſponſione ad ſingula capita,qua non tantùm ſæuitia
& impietas tam iniqui Edicti,ſed mendacia quóque,
& fraudes, & impoſturæ deteguntur,
& confutantur,

Per D. Andream Philopatrum presbyterum, ac Theologum
Romanum, ex Anglis olim oriundum.

Apoc. 17. verſ. 6.

Et vidi mulierem ebriam de ſanguine ſanctorum & de ſanguine Martyrum Ieſu.

LVGDVNI,
APVD IOANNEM DIDIER.
M. D. X C I I.

B.

14   *Reſponſio ad Edictum*
cùm faces bellorum ac ſeditionum in omnes cir-
cumquáque prouincias coniecerint , & tandem

Regine Angliæ, Sect.1.   35
calamitas.Elizabetha,quòd Dominum derelique-
ris, quod viam Regiam religionis Chriſtianæ ac

EXAMPLE 16: A. Title page B. Running title (image reduced 30 percent)

EXAMPLE 16

CATALOG RECORD

ref. no.

	100 1	Parsons, Robert, $d 1546-1610.
1,2,3,4	245 10	Elizabethae, Angliae reginae haeresin Caluinianam propugnantis, saeuissimum in Catholicos sui regni edictum : $b quod in alios qu´oque reipublicae Christianae principes, contumelias continet indignissimas : promulgatum Londini 29. Nouembris, 1591 : cum responsione ad singula capita, qua non tant`um saeuitia & impietas tam iniqui edicti, sed mendacia qu´oque, & fraudes, & imposturae deteguntur, & confutantur / $c per D. Andream Philopatrum ...
2,5,6	260	Lugduni : $b Apud Ioannem Didier, $c 1592.
7,8	300	[16], 278, [14] p. ; $c 17 cm. (8vo)
10	500	By Robert Parsons, S.J., writing under the pseudonym Andreas Philopater. Cf. Backer-Sommervogel.
9	500	Running title: Responsio ad edictum reginae Angliae.
11	500	Signatures: [dagger]^8 A-S^8 T^2.
12	510 4	Backer-Sommervogel $c VI, column 301, no. 13
12	510 4	Baudrier, H.L. Bib. lyonnaise, $c IV, p. 98-99
13	500	Includes index.
14	| LN	Contemporary limp vellum binding, printed paper label on spine, ties lacking.
	655 7	Chronicles. $2 rbgenr
	700 00	Elizabeth $b I, $c Queen of England, $d 1533-1603.
15	740 01	Responsio ad edictum reginae Angliae.
	| 755	Limp bindings (Binding) $2 rbbin
	| 755	Vellum bindings (Binding) $2 rbbin
	| 755	Printed paper labels (Binding) $2 rbbin

PRINCIPAL *DCRB* RULES ILLUSTRATED

ref. no.

1	0H, par. 2	(transcribe Latin ligature as component letters)
2	0H, par. 3	(convert to uppercase or lowercase according to AACR2; transcribe i/j and u/v according to pattern in main text)
3	1A2, par. 3	(bible verse omitted without using mark of omission)
4	1G8	(qualifications omitted from statement of responsibility)
5	4C2	(words or phrases preceding publisher statement transcribed)
6	4D2, par. 1	(roman numerals in date transcribed as arabic numerals)
7	5B3	(pagination sequence includes unnumbered pages)
8	5D1, par. 3	(format)
9	7C4	(variation in title note)
10	7C6 (1)	(authorship note; source of attribution included)
11	7C9	(signatures note; gatherings signed with unavailable characters)
12	7C14	(references to published descriptions)
13	7C16	(informal contents note)
14	7C18	(copy-specific note)
15	App. A.7C4-5	(added entry for title variant)

A.

Thierbuch/
Sehr Künstliche vnd
Wolgerissene Figuren/ von allerley
Thieren/ durch die weitberühmten Jost Amman
vnnd Hans Bocksperger/ sampt einer Beschreibung jhrer
Art/Natur vnd Eigenschafft/auch kurtzweiliger Hi-
storien/so darzu dienstlich. Menniglich zum
besten in Reimen gestellt.

Durch den Ehrnhafften vnd Wolge-
lehrten Georg Schallern von München.

Allen Kunstliebhabern zu ehren vnd sonderm
gefallen in Truck geben vnd verlegt/Durch
Sigmund Feyerabends Erben.

Mit Röm. Keys. Mayest. Freiheit.
Gedruckt zu Franckfort am Mayn/ Im Jar
M. D. LXXXXII.

B.

Gedruckt zu Franckfort am Mayn/
bey Johañ Feyerabend/in verlegung Sigmund Feyerabends Erben.

M. D. LXXXXII.

EXAMPLE 17: A. Title page B. Colophon

EXAMPLE 17

CATALOG RECORD

ref. no.

	100 1	Amman, Jost, $d 1539-1591.
1,2,3,4	245 10	Thierbuch : $b sehr k¨unstliche vnd wolgerissene Figuren, von allerley Thieren / $c durch die weitber¨uhmten Iost Amman vnnd Hans Bocksperger ; sampt einer Beschreibung jhrer Art, Natur vnd Eigenschafft, auch kurtzweiliger Historien, so darzu dienstlich ; menniglich zum besten in Reimen gestellt durch den ehrnhafften vnd wolgelehrten Georg Schallern von M¨unchen ...
1,2,3,5,6,7,8	260	Gedruckt zu Franckfort am Mayn : $b Allen Kunstliebhabern zu Ehren vnd sonderm Gefallen in Truck geben vnd verlegt, durch Sigmund Feyerabends Erben, $c im Iar 1592.
9	300	[108] leaves : $b ill. ; $c 17 cm. (4to)
10	500	Publisher statement precedes place of publication on t.p.
10	500	Colophon: Gedruckt ... bey Iohan[n] Feyerabend, in Verlegung Sigmund Feyerabends Erben, im Iar M.D.LXXXXII.
11	500	Signatures: A-Z^4 a-d^4.
12	500	Title in red and black; woodcut title vignette and 108 woodcut illustrations; initials.
12	500	Leaves printed on one side only.
13	510 4	BM STC German, 1455-1600, $c p. 783
13	510 4	VD 16 $c S 2261
14	LN	Library's copy in 19th-century cloth-backed marbled boards; imperfect: lacks leaves G1 and G4; leaf L1 repaired at lower right margin.
	700 10	Bocksberger, Hans, $d b. 1520.
	700 10	Schaller, Georg, $d 16th cent.
15	740 01	Sehr k¨unstliche vnd wolgerissene Figuren, von allerley Thieren.

PRINCIPAL *DCRB* RULES ILLUSTRATED

ref. no.

1	0E, par. 12	(virgule transcribed as comma)
2	0H, par. 3	(convert to uppercase or lowercase according to AACR2; transcribe i/j and u/v according to pattern in main text)
3	0H, par. 5	(gothic capitals J and U treated as I and V)
4	1G14, par. 2	(phrase transcribed after statement of responsibility; punctuated as subsequent statement of responsibility)
5	4B2	(words or phrases associated with place name transcribed)
6	4C2	(words or phrases preceding publisher statement transcribed)
7	4D1	(phrase in date transcribed)
8	4D2, par. 1	(roman numerals in date transcribed as arabic numerals)
9	5B1, par. 1	(leaves printed on one side only)
10	7C8	(publication note)
11	7C9	(signatures note)
12	7C10	(physical description note)
13	7C14	(references to published descriptions)
14	7C18	(copy-specific note)
15	App. A.7C4-5	(added entries for title variants and other titles)

Continentur hic
OPERE

1. Grotii Grolla.
2. Winsemii expeditio Belgica, poetice.
3. Epigrammata Americana Böderseii.
4. Morelse Panegyricus in Principem
   Wilhelmum.
5. R. Neuhusii Oratio inaug. Lect. publicariae
   Alcmaria.
6. ~~Erasmii~~ Pax Perpetua.
7. Timidus Auriacus D'Amour.
8. Corvinus in obitum C. BARLÆI.
9. Cabeljavii inauguratio Amstelodami.
10. Jus Successionis in Palatinatum.

EXAMPLE 18: Manuscript contents leaf of vol. 1 (image reduced 15 percent)

EXAMPLE 18

CATALOG RECORD

ref. no.

1	245 00	[Pamphlets and printed ephemera concerning the Dutch Wars of Independence]
2	260	$c 1602-1648.
3,4	300	ca. 500 pieces in 23 v. : $b ill. ; $c 16-29 cm.
5	500	A collection of pamphlets, broadsides, engravings and other printed material in Latin, Dutch and French, printed at various places in France and the Low Countries between 1602 and 1648; primarily concerning the Dutch Wars of Independence, but also including addresses on a variety of unrelated subjects, funeral orations and miscellaneous official decrees.
6	500	Title devised by cataloger.
7	500	Each volume has manuscript contents leaf in Latin.
7	500	Bound uniformly in contemporary blind tooled vellum.
	655 7	Addresses $z Netherlands $y 17th century. $2 rbgenr
	655 7	Broadsides $z Netherlands $y 17th century. $2 rbgenr
	655 7	Ephemera $z Netherlands $y 17th century. $2 rbgenr
	655 7	Funeral addresses $z Netherlands $y 17th century. $2 rbgenr
	655 7	Proclamations $z Netherlands $y 17th century. $2 rbgenr
	755	Blind tooled bindings (Binding) $z Netherlands $y 17th century. $2 rbbin
	755	Vellum bindings (Binding) $z Netherlands $y 17th century. $2 rbbin

PRINCIPAL *DCRB* RULES ILLUSTRATED

ref. no.

1	1B5	(title devised from content of work)
2	4A6	(unpublished collection: place and publisher statements omitted from publication area)
3	5B18	(term "pieces" used in statement of extent to designate items of varying character)
4	5D3	(volumes of a multivolume set vary in size)
5	7C1	(nature, scope or artistic form note)
6	7C3	(source of title proper note)
7	7C10	(physical description note)

ʹINSTRVCCION
DE SACERDOTES,
Y SVMA DE CASOS
DE CONCIENCIA.

COMPVESTA POR EL REVERENDISSIMO SEÑOR
Cardenal Francisco Toledo, Religioso de la Compañia
de IESVS.

Con las Addiciones y Anotaciones de Andres Victorelo, puestas
al fin de cada Capitulo, y añadido el Tratado del
Sacramento de la Orden.

TRADVZIDA DE LATIN EN CASTELLANO,
por el Dotor Diego Henrriquez de Salas.

Corregida y emendada en esta segunda impression por el Padre Iuan de
Salas de la Compañia de IESVS.

Con Indices y Sumarios copiosissimos de nueuo corregidos.

Año   1611.

EN BARCELO

Por Sebastiañ Matev

Acosta de I

EXAMPLE 19: Title page

EXAMPLE 19

CATALOG RECORD

ref. no.

	100 1	Toledo, Francisco de, $d 1532-1596.
	240 10	De instructione sacerdotum. $l Spanish
2,3,4,5,6	245 10	Instruccion de sacerdotes, y suma de casos de conciencia / $c compuesta por el reuerendissimo se~nor cardenal Francisco Toledo, religioso de la Compa~nia de Iesus ; con las addiciones y anotaciones de Andres Victorelo, puestas al fin de cada capitulo, y a~nadido el Tratado del sacramento de la orden ; traduzida de latin en castellano por el dotor Diego Henrriquez de Salas.
2,3,7,8,9	250	Corregida y emendada en esta segunda impression / $b por el padre Iuan de Salas de la Compa~nia de Iesus, con indices y sumarios copiosissimos de nueuo corregidos.
1,3,10,11,12,13	260	En Barcelo[na] : $b Por Sebastian Mateu[...] : Acosta de Iu[...], $c a~no 1621.
14,15,16	300	[8], 1080, [48+] p. ; $c 22 cm. (4to)
21	500	Description based on imperfect copy: lacks lower right portion of title page, and all after p. [48] of 3rd group.
17	500	Translation of: De instructione sacerdotum.
18	LN	Signatures: [sec.]^4 A-3X^8 3Y^4 a-f^4 (Extent of Loyola's copy).
19	500	Title vignette (Jesuit device); initials.
20	500	"Addicion a la suma de Toledo, que trata del sacramento del orden. Por el padre Martin Fornario de la Compa~nia de Iesus": p. 1053-1080.
	700 12	Fornari, Martino, $d 1547-1612. $t De sacramento ordinis. $l Spanish. $f 1621.
	700 10	Salas, Juan de, $d 1553-1612.
	700 20	Henrriquez de Salas, Diego.
	700 10	Victorelo, Andres.

PRINCIPAL *DCRB* RULES ILLUSTRATED

ref. no.

1	0B2	(imperfect copy; no reliable description of missing text available)
2	0H, par. 1	(accents not added to "instruccion," "Iesus," etc.)
3	0H, par. 3	(convert to uppercase or lowercase according to AACR2; transcribe i/j and u/v according to pattern in main text)
4	1G6	(multiple statements of responsibility)
5	1G7	(title of address in statement of responsibility)
6	1G8	(qualifications retained in statement of responsibility)
7	2B1	(words or phrases associated with edition statement transcribed)
8	2B3	(phrase referring to impression treated as edition statement)
9	2C1	(statement of responsibility relating to edition)
10	4B2	(words or phrases associated with place name transcribed)
11	4C2	(words or phrases preceding publisher statement transcribed)
12	4C6, par. 1	(multiple publisher statements separated by prescribed punctuation)
13	4D1	(phrase in date transcribed)
14	5B3	(pagination sequence includes unnumbered pages)
15	5B12	(incomplete copy; no reliable description of extent available)
16	5D1, par. 3	(format)
17	7C2	(language of publication note; translation)
18	7C9	(signatures note; gatherings signed with unavailable characters)
19	7C10	(physical description note)
20	7C16	(informal contents note)
21	7C18	(note relating to imperfect copy, where no reliable description of missing elements available)

J. DE BRUNES
NIEVWE WYN
IN OUDE
LE'ER-ZACKEN.

Bevvijzende in Spreeck-vvoor-
den, 't vernuft der menschen,
ende 't gheluck van onze Neder-
landsche Taek.

SPE
&
METV

TOT MIDDELBVRGH,

By *Zacharias Roman*, Boeck-ver-
cooper, op den Burght, inden Ver-
gulden Bybel. *Anno 1636.*

TOT MIDDELBVRGH,

Gedruckt by *Hans vander Hellen,*
Boeck-drucker, op de groote Marĉt.
ANNO 1636.

I. De Brunes	I	Spreeck-woorden.
en vanght de wespen niet,		De kraeyen gaetmen licht voor-by

EXAMPLE 20: A. Title page **B.** Colophon **C.** Running title

EXAMPLE 20

CATALOG RECORD

ref. no.

	100	1	Brune, Johan de, $d 1588-1658.
	240	10	Nieuwe wyn in oude le'er-zacken
1,2	245	10	I. de Brunes Nieuwe wyn in oude le'er-zacken : $b bevvijzende in spreeck-vvoorden, 't vernuft der menschen, ende 't gheluck van onze nederlandsche taele.
1,3,4,5,6	260		Tot Middelburgh : $b By Zacharias Roman ... : $b Gedruckt by Hans vander Hellen ..., $c anno 1636.
7,8	300		[24], 496, [8] p. ; $c 14 cm. (12mo)
9	500		Running title: I. de Brunes Spreeck-woorden.
10	500		Printer statement from colophon.
11	500		Signatures: A-Y^{12}.
12	500		Title vignette (publisher's device); initials; tail-pieces.
13	500		Includes index.
14	|	LN	Library's copy in old vellum.
15	740	01	J. de Brunes Nieuwe wyn in oude le'er-zacken.
16	740	01	Nieuwe wyn in oude le'er-zacken.
17	740	01	I. de Brunes Spreeck-woorden.
|	755		Vellum bindings (Binding) $2 rbbin

PRINCIPAL *DCRB* RULES ILLUSTRATED

ref. no.

1	0H, par. 3	(convert to uppercase or lowercase according to AACR2; transcribe i/j and u/v according to pattern in main text)
2	1B1	(statement of responsibility inseparably linked to title proper)
3	4B2	(words or phrases associated with place name transcribed)
4	4C2	(words or phrases preceding publisher statements transcribed; addresses omitted)
5	4C6, par. 2	(multiple publisher statements in more than one source)
6	4D1	(phrase in date transcribed)
7	5B3	(pagination sequence includes unnumbered pages)
8	5D1, par. 3	(format)
9	7C4	(variations in title note)
10	7C8	(publication note)
11	7C9	(signatures note)
12	7C10	(physical description note)
13	7C16	(informal contents note)
14	7C18	(copy-specific note)
15	App. A.0H	(added entry for title proper in modern orthography)
16	App. A.1B1	(added entry for chief title)
17	App. A.7C4-5	(added entry for title variant)

VALERI ANDREAE

DESSELI I.C.

BIBLIOTHECA BELGICA:

DE BELGIS VITA SCRIPTISQ. CLARIS.

PRAEMISSA

TOPOGRAPHICA

BELGII TOTIVS SEV

GERMANIAE INFERIORIS

DESCRIPTIONE.

Editio renovata, & tertiâ parte auctior.

LOVANII

Typis IACOBI ZEGERS, cIↄ. Iↄc. XLIII.

Cum Privilegio Regis.

EXAMPLE 21: Title page

EXAMPLE 21

CATALOG RECORD

ref. no.

	100 1	Andreas, Valerius, $d 1588-1655.
	240 10	Bibliotheca Belgica
1,2,3,4,13	245 10	ValerI Andreae DesselI I.C. Bibliotheca Belgica : $b de Belgis vita scriptisq. claris. praemissa topographica Belgii totius seu Germaniae inferioris descriptione.
5	250	Editio renovata, & terti^a parte auctior.
6	260	Lovanii : $b Typis Iacobi Zegers, $c 1643.
7	300	[16], 110, [22], 900 p. ; $c 20 cm. (4to)
8	500	Signatures: $*^4$ $2*^4$ $A-O^4$ a^4 b^6, $^2A-5V^4$ $5X^2$.
9	500	Engravings: title vignette (printer's device); coat of arms on t.p. verso.
9	500	Title in red and black; initials.
10	LN	Library's copy in modern calf-backed boards; bookplate of John Webster Spargo.
	LAE	Spargo, John Webster, $d 1896-1956, $e former owner.
	700 10	Zegers, Jacob, $e printer.
11	740 01	Valerii Andreae Desselii I.C. Bibliotheca Belgica.
12	740 01	Bibliotheca Belgica.
	755	Donors' bookplates (Provenance) $z United States $y 20th century. $2 rbprov

PRINCIPAL *DCRB* RULES ILLUSTRATED

ref. no.

1	0H, par. 4	(capital I [=ii] not converted to lowercase)
2	0K, par. 1	(initials transcribed without internal spaces)
3	1B1	(statement of responsibility inseparably linked to title proper)
4	1G8	(qualifications retained in statement of responsibility)
5	2B1	(words or phrases associated with edition statement transcribed)
6	4C2	(words or phrases preceding publisher statement transcribed)
7	5D1, par. 3	(format)
8	7C9	(signatures note)
9	7C10	(physical description note)
10	7C18	(copy-specific note)
11	App. A.0J2	(added entry for title proper with expansion of contraction)
12	App. A.1B1	(added entry for chief title)
13	App. B	(capital I [=ii] not converted to lowercase)

L'ALCORAN
De

MAHOMET.
Translaté d'Arabe en François,

PAR LE
SIEVR DV RYER
Sieur de la Garde Malezair.

2160

Iouxte la Copie imprimée
à PARIS,
Chez Antoine de Sommaville,

CIƆIƆCXLIX. 1649.
Auec Priuilege du Roy.

EXAMPLE 22: Title page

EXAMPLE 22

CATALOG RECORD

ref. no.

	130 0	Koran. $l French. $f 1649.
1	245 12	L'Alcoran de Mahomet / $c translat´e d'arabe en fran.cois, par le sieur du Ryer, sieur de la Garde Malezair ; iouxte la copie imprim´ee `a Paris, chez Antoine de Sommaville.
2,3,4,5	260	[Amsterdam : $b Josse Jansson], $c 1649.
6	300	[12], 416, [4] p. ; $c 13 cm. (12mo)
7,8	500	Printed in Amsterdam by Josse Jansson; the text is that of the 1647 Paris edition. Cf. Rahir.
9	500	Signatures: *^{6} A-R^{12} s^6.
10	500	Title in red and black.
11	510 4	Rahir, E. Les Elzevier, $c 2019
12	500	Errata: p. [420].
13	| LN	Library's copy in old vellum; inscription on front flyleaf signed "Jean Josse Schelhofer le jeune," dated 1696; inscription on t.p. dated 1724; stamps of West Baden College.
	700 10	Du Ryer, Andr´e, $d ca. 1580-ca. 1660.
	| LAE	Schelhofer, Jean Josse, $e former owner.
	| LAE	West Baden College, $e former owner.

PRINCIPAL *DCRB* RULES ILLUSTRATED

ref. no.

1	1G14, par. 2	(phrase transcribed after statement of responsibility; punctuated as subsequent statement of responsibility)
2	4B1	(supplied place of publication given in English form)
3	4B10	(place of publication supplied from reference source)
4	4C8	(publisher supplied from reference source)
5	4D2, par. 1	(roman numerals in date transcribed as arabic numerals)
6	5B3	(pagination sequence includes unnumbered pages)
7	7C7	(edition and bibliographic history note)
8	7C8	(publication note)
9	7C9	(signatures note)
10	7C10	(physical description note)
11	7C14	(references to published descriptions)
12	7C16	(informal contents note)
13	7C18	(copy-specific note)

A.

B.

EXAMPLE 23: A. Title page B. Publication date expressed as chronogram at end of preface

EXAMPLE 23

CATALOG RECORD

ref. no.

	100 1	Schott, Gaspar, \$d 1608-1666.
1,2,3,4	245 10	Ioco-seriorum naturae et artis, siue, Magiae naturalis centuriae tres / \$c auctore Aspasio Caramuelio ; accessit Diattibe [sic] de prodigiosis crucibus.
5,6,7	260	[W¨urzburg : \$b s.n., \$c 1666]
8,9	300	[4], 363, [9] p., 22 leaves of plates (some folded) : \$b ill. (engravings) ; \$c 22 cm. (4to)
10,11	500	By Gaspar Schott, S.J.; author and probable place of publication from Backer-Sommervogel.
11	500	Imprint date at end of preface, expressed as chronogram: Me ergo frVere aC DIV VaLe.
12	500	Signatures: $)(^2$ A-2Y^4 2z^2 [sec.]^4.
13	500	Engraved t.p.; initials; head- and tail-pieces.
13	500	The phrase "auctore Aspasio Caramuelio" is stamped on the engraved title page.
14	510 4	Backer-Sommervogel, \$c VII, column 911, no. 3
15	500	"Athanasij Kircheri Soc. Iesu Diatribe de prodigiosis crucibus ...": p. [307]-363.
16	LN	Library's copy in old calf, rebacked; imperfect: lacks plate 15.
	655 7	Scientific recreations. \$2 rbgenr
	700 12	Kircher, Athanasius, \$d 1602-1680. \$t Diatribe de prodigiosis crucibus. \$f 1666.
17	740 01	Joco-seriorum naturae et artis, sive, Magiae naturalis centuriae tres.
18	740 01	Magiae naturalis centuriae tres.
19	740 01	Diatribe de prodigiosis crucibus.
	755	Chronograms (Publishing) \$2 rbpub

PRINCIPAL *DCRB* RULES ILLUSTRATED

ref. no.

1	0G	(misprint transcribed as it appears)
2	0H, par. 2	(transcribe Latin ligature as component letters)
3	0H, par. 3	(convert to uppercase or lowercase according to AACR2; transcribe i/j and u/v according to pattern in main text)
4	1B3	(title proper inclusive of alternative title)
5	4B12	(probable place of publication supplied)
6	4C9	(publisher unknown)
7	4D2, par. 2	(date expressed as chronogram)
8	5C1	(illustrations; **option:** describe graphic process or technique)
9	5D1, par. 3	(format)
10	7C6 (1)	(authorship note)
11	7C8	(publication note)
12	7C9	(signatures note)
13	7C10	(physical description note)
14	7C14	(references to published descriptions)
15	7C16	(informal contents note)
16	7C18	(copy-specific note)
17	App. A.0H	(added entry for title proper in modern orthography)
18	App. A.1B3	(added entry for alternative title)
19	App. A.1E1-2	(added entry for title of additional work)

AN EXACT

Abridgment

Of all the

STATUTES

IN

FORCE and USE

From the beginning of

MAGNA CHARTA.

Begun by *Edmund Wingate* of *Grays-Inn* Esq;
and since continued under their proper Titles
Alphabetically down to the Year 1689.

In this Impreſſion the *Year* of the *King*, and the *Chapter*
of every *Act of Parliament* have been compared with the *Statute-*
Book at large; wherein many hundreds of falſe References are
Corrected with great Exactneſs and Care, to prevent the
Reader's being miſled as he hath been in the former Editions.

With a more compleat and exact Table then was before.

LONDON,

Printed by the Aſſigns ⎰ ⎱ And by the Aſſigns of *R. At-*
of the King's Printers. ⎱ ⎰ *kins* and *E. Atkins* Eſquires

And to be ſold by *Charles Harper,* *William Crooke,* and *Richard Tonſon,*
at the *Flower-de-lace* in *Fleetſtreet,* at the *Green-Dragon* without
Temple-Bar, and within *Grays-Inn-Gate* next *Grays-Inn-Lane.* 1689.

EXAMPLE 24: Title page

EXAMPLE 24

CATALOG RECORD

ref. no.

	100 1	Wingate, Edmund, $d 1596-1656.
1,2	245 13	An exact abridgment of all the statutes in force and use from the beginning of Magna Charta / $c begun by Edmund Wingate ... ; and since continued under their proper titles alphabetically down to the year 1689.
3,4,5	250	In this impression the year of the King, and the chapter of every Act of Parliament have been compared with the statute-book at large, wherein many hundreds of false references are corrected with great exactness and care, to prevent the reader's being misled as he hath been in the former editions, with a more compleat and exact table then was before.
6,7,8	260	London : $b Printed by the assigns of the King's printers, and by the assigns of R. Atkins and E. Atkins Esquires, and to be sold by Charles Harper, William Crooke, and Richard Tonson ..., $c 1689.
9,10,11	300	[4], 696 [i.e. 694], [58] p. ; $c 19 cm. (8vo)
12	500	Preface signed: J. Washington.
13	500	Signatures: A^2 B-3B^8.
14	500	Title within double rule.
15	500	Includes index.
16	LN	Contemporary blind-tooled full calf binding.
	655 7	Legal works $z England $y 17th century. $2 rbgenr
	700 10	Washington, Joseph, $d d. 1694.
	755	Blind tooled bindings (Binding) $2 rbbin
	755	Calf bindings (Binding) $2 rbbin

PRINCIPAL *DCRB* RULES ILLUSTRATED

ref. no.

1	1G8	(qualifications omitted from statement of responsibility)
2	1G14, par. 2	(phrase transcribed after statement of responsibility; punctuated as subsequent statement of responsibility)
3	2B1	(words or phrases associated with edition statement transcribed)
4	2B3	(phrase referring to impression treated as edition statement)
5	2C1	(statement of responsibility relating to edition does not name person; prescribed punctuation not used)
6	4C1	(publisher statement includes printers and booksellers)
7	4C2	(words or phrases preceding publisher statement transcribed; addresses omitted)
8	4C6, par. 1	(multiple publishers linked by connecting words; no prescribed punctuation)
9	5B3	(pagination sequence includes unnumbered pages)
10	5B7, par. 2	(error in paging corrected)
11	5D1, par. 3	(format)
12	7C6 (2)	(other statements of responsibility note)
13	7C9	(signatures note)
14	7C10	(physical description note)
15	7C16	(informal contents note)
16	7C18	(copy-specific note)

RENATI DES CARTES
GEOMETRIA,

Unà cum Notis

FLORIMONDI DE BEAUNE,

In Curia Blesensi Consiliarii Regii, & Commentariis illustrata,

Operâ atque studio

FRANCISCI à SCHOOTEN,

in Acad. Lugd. Batav. Matheseos Professoris.

AB EODEM DUM VIVERET DILIGENTER RECOGNITA,
locupletioribus Commentariis instructa, multisque egregiis accessionibus, tam
ad uberiorem explicationem, quàm ad amplificandam hujus Geometriæ
excellentiam facientibus exornata.

Nunc verò à Viro Clariss. denuo revisa, & ab innumeris mendis, quibus priores Editiones scatebant, repurgata, una cum notis quibusdam & animadversionibus tumultuariis in universum Opus, huic quartæ editioni recens adjectis,

Accedit insuper

COMPENDIUM MUSICÆ.

Cum Gratia & Privilegio Sacræ Cæs. Majest.

FRANCOFVRTI AD MOENVM,
Sumptibus FRIDERICI KNOCHII, Bibliop.

Anno M DC XCV.

EXAMPLE 25: Title page

EXAMPLE 25

CATALOG RECORD

ref. no.

	100 1	Descartes, Ren´e, \$d 1596-1650.
	240 10	G´eom´etrie. \$l Latin
1,2,3,4,5,6	245 10	Renati Des Cartes Geometria : \$b un`a cum notis Florimondi de Beaune, in curia Blesensi consiliarii regii, & commentariis illustrata, oper^a atque studio Francisci `a Schooten ... : ab eodem dum viveret diligenter recognita, locupletioribus commentariis instructa, multisque egregiis accessionibus, tam ad ulteriorem explicationem, qu`am ad ampliandam hujus Geometriae excellentiam facientibus exornata.
1,2,7,8,9	250	Nunc ver`o `a viro clariss. denuo revisa, & ab innumeris mendis, quibus priores editiones scatebant, repurgata, un`a cum notis quibusdam & animadversionibus tumultuariis in universum opus, huic quartae editioni recens adjectis, accedit insuper Compendium musicae.
10	260	Francofurti ad Moenum : \$b Sumptibus Friderici Knochii, bibliop., \$c anno 1695.
11,12	300	[16], 520, 48, [8], 468 p. : \$b ill. ; \$c 22 cm. (4to)
13	500	Translation of: G´eom´etrie; issued with other works in Latin (not necessarily in translation).
14	LN	Signatures: *-2*^{2} 2[star]^4 A-3T^4. (Extent of Duke's copy).
15	LN	Imperfect copy: all after p. 520 lacking.
15	LN	Misbound: p. [3]-[6] bound after p. [7]-[8] (1st group).
	700 10	Beaune, Florimond de, \$d 1601-1652.
	700 10	Schooten, Frans van, \$d 1615-1660.
	700 12	Descartes, Ren´e, \$d 1596-1650. \$t Musicae compendium. \$f 1695.
16	740 01	Geometria.
17	740 01	Musicae compendium.
17	740 01	Compendium musicae.

PRINCIPAL *DCRB* RULES ILLUSTRATED

ref. no.

1	0H, par. 2	(transcribe Latin ligature as component letters)
2	0H, par. 3	(convert to uppercase or lowercase according to AACR2; transcribe i/j and u/v according to pattern in main text)
3	1B1	(statement of responsibility inseparably linked to title proper)
4	1D2, par. 1	(other titles or phrases following title proper treated as other title information)
5	1D5	(other title information with inseparable statements of responsibility)
6	1G8	(qualifications omitted from statement of responsibility)
7	2B1	(words or phrases associated with edition statement transcribed)
8	2C1	(statement of responsibility relating to edition does not name person; prescribed punctuation not used)
9	2C3	(phrases following edition statement)
10	4D1	(phrase in date transcribed)
11	5B6	(multiple sequences of numbering)
12	5D1, par. 3	(format)
13	7C2	(language of publication note; translation)
14	7C9	(signatures note; gatherings signed with unavailable characters)
15	7C18	(copy-specific note)
16	App. A.1B1	(added entry for chief title)
17	App. A.1E1-2	(added entry for title of additional work)

Tyrannick Love;

OR, THE

Royal Martyr.

A

TRAGEDY.

As it is Acted by His Majesty's Servants at the

THEATRE ROYAL.

By *JOHN DRYDEN*, Servant to His Majesty.

Non jam prima peto——neq; vincere certo;
Extremum rediisse pudet.—— Virg.

LONDON,

Printed for *Henry Herringman*, and are to be sold by
R. Bently, J. Tonson, F. Saunders, and *T. Bennet*. 1695.

EXAMPLE 26A: Title page

EXAMPLE 26A

CATALOG RECORD

ref. no.

	100 1	Dryden, John, $d 1631-1700.
1	245 10	Tyrannick love, or, The royal martyr : $b a tragedy : as it is acted by His Majesty's servants at the Theatre Royal / $c by John Dryden, servant to His Majesty.
2,3	260	London : $b Printed for Henry Herringman, and are to be sold by R. Bently, J. Tonson, F. Saunders, and T. Bennet, $c 1695.
4,5,6	300	[10], 58 [i.e. 57], [1] p. ; $c 23 cm. (4to)
7	500	Wing calls this the 5th ed.
9	500	Error in paging: no. 55 omitted.
8	500	Signatures: A-H^4 I^2.
10	510 4	Wing (2nd ed.) $c D2397
10	510 4	Macdonald, H. Dryden, $c 74e
11	LN	No. 2 in a vol. with binder's title: Seventeenth-century plays.
12	740 01	Tyrannick love.
12	740 01	Royal martyr.
13	LTE	Seventeenth-century plays.

PRINCIPAL *DCRB* RULES ILLUSTRATED

ref. no.

1	1A1, par. 4	(colon precedes each unit of other title information)
2	4C1	(publisher statement includes booksellers)
3	4C2	(words or phrases preceding publisher statement transcribed)
4	5B3	(pagination sequence includes unnumbered pages)
5	5B7, par. 2	(error in paging corrected)
6	5D1, par. 3	(format)
7	7C7	(edition and bibliographic history note)
8	7C9	(signatures note)
9	7C10	(physical description note)
10	7C14	(references to published descriptions)
11	7C18	(copy-specific note)
12	App. A.1B3	(added entry for alternative title)
13	App. A.7C18	(added entry for copy-specific title: binder's title)

Tyrannick Love;

OR, THE

Royal Martyr.

A

TRAGEDY.

As it is Acted by His Majesty's Servants at the

THEATRE ROYAL.

By *JOHN DRYDEN*, Servant to His Majesty.

Non jam prima peto——neq; vincere certo;
Extremum rediisse pudet.—— Virg.

LONDON,

Printed for *Henry Herringman*, and are to be sold by
R. Bently, J. Tonson, F. Saunders, and *T. Bennet.* 1695.

EXAMPLE 26B: Title page

EXAMPLE 26B

CATALOG RECORD USING DOUBLE PUNCTUATION

ref. no.

	100	1	Dryden, John, $d 1631-1700.
1,2	245	10	Tyrannick love; or, The royal martyr. : $b A tragedy. : As it is acted by His Majesty's servants at the Theatre Royal. / $c By John Dryden, servant to His Majesty..
3,4	260		London, : $b Printed for Henry Herringman, and are to be sold by R. Bently, J. Tonson, F. Saunders, and T. Bennet., $c 1695..
5,6,7	300		[10], 58 [i.e. 57], [1] p. ; $c 23 cm. (4to)
8	500		Wing calls this the 5th ed.
10	500		Error in paging: no. 55 omitted.
9	500		Signatures: A-H^4 I^2.
11	510	4	Wing (2nd ed.) $c D2397
11	510	4	Macdonald, H. Dryden, $c 74e
12	|	LN	No. 2 in a vol. with binder's title: Seventeenth-century plays.
13	740	01	Tyrannick love.
13	740	01	Royal martyr.
14	|	LTE	Seventeenth-century plays.

PRINCIPAL *DCRB* RULES ILLUSTRATED

ref. no.

1	0E, par. 5	(**option**: double punctuation)
2	1A1, par. 4	(colon precedes each unit of other title information)
3	4C1	(publisher statement includes booksellers)
4	4C2	(words or phrases preceding publisher statement transcribed)
5	5B3	(pagination sequence includes unnumbered pages)
6	5B7, par. 2	(error in paging corrected)
7	5D1, par. 3	(format)
8	7C7	(edition and bibliographic history note)
9	7C9	(signatures note)
10	7C10	(physical description note)
11	7C14	(references to published descriptions)
12	7C18	(copy-specific note)
13	App. A.1B3	(added entry for alternative title)
14	App. A.7C18	(added entry for copy-specific title: binder's title)

The Famous Flower of Serving-men;

Or, The Lady turn'd Serving-man.

YOU beauteous ladies, great and small,
I write unto you one and all,
Whereby that you may understand
What I have suffer'd in this land.

I was by birth a lady fair,
My father's chief and only heir,
But when my good old father died,
Then was I made a young knight's bride.

And then my love built me a bower,
Bedeck'd with many a fragrant flower;
A braver bower you ne'er did see
Than my true love did build for me.

But there came thieves late in the night,
Who robb'd my bower and slew my knight,
And after that my knight was slain,
I could no longer there remain.

My servants all did from me fly
In the midst of my extremity,

And left me by myself alone,
With heart more cold than any stone.

Yet though my heart was full of care,
Heaven would not suffer me to despair,
Therefore in haste I chang'd my name,
From Fair Elise to Sweet William.

And therewithall I cut my hair,
And drest myself in man's attire,
My doublet, hose, and beaver hat,
And a golden band about my neck,

With a silver rapier by my side;
So like a gallant I did ride:
The thing I did delight upon,
It was to be a serving-man.

Thus in my sumptuous man's array,
I bravely rode along the way;
And at the last it chanced so
That I to the King's court did go:

Then to the King I bow'd full low,
My love and duty for to show;
And so much favour I did crave,
That I a serving-man's place might have.

Stand up, brave youth, the King reply'd,
Thy service shall be not be deny'd;
But tell me first what thou canst do,
Thou shalt be fitted thereunto.

Wilt thou be usher of my hall,
To wait upon my nobles all?
Or wilt thou be taster of my wine,
To wait upon me when I dine?

Or wilt thou be my chamberlain,
To make my bed both soft and fine?
Or wilt thou be one of my guard,
And I will give thee thy reward.

Sweet William, with a smiling face,
Said to the King, If it please your grace
To show such favour unto me,
Your chamberlain I fain would be.

The King did then his nobles call,
To ask the counsel of them all;
Who gave consent Sweet William he
The King's own chamberlain should be.

Now mark what strange things came to pass,
As the King one day hunting was
With all his lords and noble train,
Sweet William did alone remain.

Sweet William had no company then
With him at home, but an old man;
And when he saw the house was clear,
He took a lute which he had there:

Upon the lute Sweet William play'd,
And to the same he sung and said,
With a sweet and noble voice,
Which made the old man to rejoice.

"My father was as brave a lord
"As ever Europe did afford,

"My mother was a lady bright,
"My husband was a valiant knight,
"And I myself a lady gay,
"Bedeck'd with gorgeous rich array;
"The bravest lady in the land
"Had not more pleasure at command.

"I had my music every day,
"Harmonious lessons for to play;
"I had my virgins fair and free,
"Continually to wait on me.

"But now, alas! my husband's dead,
"And all my friends are from me fled,
"My former joys are past and gone,
"For I am now a serving-man."

At last the King from hunting came,
And presently upon the same
He called for this good old man,
And thus to speak the King began.

What news, what news, old man? quoth he,
What news hast thou to tell to me?
Brave news! the old man he did say,
Sweet William is a lady gay.

If this be true thou tellest me,
I'll make thee a lord of high degree;
But if thy words do prove a lye,
Thou shalt be hang'd up presently.

But when the King the truth had found,
His joys did more and more abound;
According as the old man did say,
Sweet William prov'd a lady gay.

Therefore the King, without delay,
Put on her glorious rich array,
And on her head a crown of gold,
Which was most glorious to behold.

And then, for fear of further strife,
He took Sweet William for his wife:
The like before was never seen,
A Serving-man became a Queen.

Printed and sold by *J. Butler*, in *High-Street*, *Worcester*. Sold also by *G. Lewis*, in *Broad Street*, *Worcester*; and by *S. Hazell*, in *Bolt Lane*, *Gloucester*.

EXAMPLE 27: Single-sheet publication (image reduced 50 percent)

EXAMPLE 27

CATALOG RECORD

ref. no.

1,2,3	245 04	The Famous flower of serving-men, or, The lady turn'd serving-man.
4,5,6,7,8,9,10	260	[Worcester, England] : $b Printed and sold by J. Butler, in High-Street, Worcester, sold also by G. Lewis, in Broad Street, Worcester, and by S. Hazell, in Bolt Lane, Glocester, $c [ca. 1705]
11,12,13	300	1 sheet ([1] p.) : $b 2 ill. ; $c 24 x 32 cm.
14,15	500	In verse; begins: You beauteous ladies, great and small.
16	500	An earlier ed. ([1683?] Wing F369A) was signed: L.P. Authorship attributed to Laurence Price by Dr. David Harker in a letter to the Beinecke Library.
17	500	J. Butler was a bookseller in Worcester, 1702-1708. Cf. Plomer, H.R. Dict. of printers and booksellers who were at work in England, Scotland, and Ireland from 1668 to 1725.
18	510 4	ESTC $c n048885
	700 00	L. P. $q (Laurence Price), $d fl. 1625-1680?
	700 10	Butler, John, $d fl. 1702-1708, $e printer.
	700 10	Lewis, G., $e bookseller.
	700 10	Hazell, S., $e bookseller.
19	740 01	Lady turn'd serving-man.
20	740 01	Lady turned serving-man.
21	740 01	You beauteous ladies, great and small.

PRINCIPAL *DCRB* RULES ILLUSTRATED

ref. no.

1	0D	(prescribed sources of information for single-sheet publication)
2	1B3	(title proper inclusive of alternative title)
3	1F2	(begin transcription of single sheet publications with first line of printing)
4	4B8	(place of publication appears only as part of another area; supplied in modern English form)
5	4C1	(publisher statement includes printer and booksellers)
6	4C2	(words or phrases preceding publisher statement transcribed; **option:** address included)
7	4C3	(place of publication transcribed as part of publisher statement)
8	4C6, par. 1	(multiple publishers linked by connecting words; no prescribed punctuation)
9	4D5	(conjectural date based on address of printer)
10	4D6	(date uncertain; "approximate date" pattern used)
11	5B15	(pagination statement for single-sheet publications)
12	5C4	(number of illustrations)
13	5D5	(size of single-sheet publications)
14	7C1	(nature, scope or artistic form note)
15	7C4	(variation in title note)
16	7C6 (1)	(authorship note; source of attribution included)
17	7C8	(publication note)
18	7C14	(references to published descriptions)
19	App. A.0H	(added entry for title proper in modern orthography)
20	App. A.1B3	(added entry for alternative title)
21	App. A.7C4-5	(added entry for other title)

JOH. ALPHONSI TURRETINI

Paſtoris, S. Theol. & Hiſt. Ecclesiast.
Profeſſoris, Academiæ p. t. Rectoris,

DE VARIIS

CHRISTIANÆ

DOCTRINÆ FATIS,

ORATIO ACADEMICA,

Dicta ſtatis A C A D E M I Æ G E N E V E N S I S
Solennibus, XI. *Mai. An.* M. DCCVIII.

An UNIVERSITY

ORATION

Concerning the

DIFFERENT FATES

OF THE

Chriſtian RELIGION.

Spoke in the publick Act of the UNIVERSITY *of* GENEVA,
the Eleventh Day of May, *A. D.* M. DCCVIII.

By J O H N A L P H O N S U S T U R R E T I N, *Paſtor, Pro-
feſſor of Divinity and Eccleſiaſtical Hiſtory, and Deputy
Rector of the* UNIVERSITY.

LONDON
Printed: and Re-printed at *Edinburgh* by *James Watſon*, to be Sold at
his Shop next the *Red-Lion*, oppoſite to the *Lucken-Booths.* 1709.

EXAMPLE 28: Title page

EXAMPLE 28

CATALOG RECORD

ref. no.

	100 1	Turrettini, Jean Alphonse, $d 1671-1737.
	240 10	De variis Christianae doctrinae fatis, oratio academica. $l English & Latin
1,2,3,4,5,	245 10	Joh. Alphonsi Turretini pastoris, s. theol. & hist. ecclesiast. professoris ...
6,7,8,9		De variis Christianae doctrinae fatis, oratio academica ... = $b An university oration concerning the different fates of the Christian religion ... / $c by John Alphonsus Turretin ...
2,10,11,12,13	260	[Edinburgh] : $b London printed and re-printed at Edinburgh by James Watson, to be sold at his shop next the Red-Lion, opposite to the Lucken-Booths, $c 1709.
14,15	300	[4], 35, [1] p. ; $c 24 cm. (4to)
16	500	"Spoke in the publick act of the University of Geneva, the eleventh day of May, A.D. M.DCCVIII."
17	500	Latin and English texts in parallel columns.
	655 7	Addresses. $2 rbgenr
18	740 01	De variis Christianae doctrinae fatis, oratio academica.
19	740 01	University oration concerning the different fates of the Christian religion.

PRINCIPAL *DCRB* RULES ILLUSTRATED

ref. no.

1	0H, par. 2	(transcribe Latin ligature as component letters)
2	0H, par. 3	(convert to uppercase or lowercase according to AACR2; transcribe i/j and u/v according to pattern in main text)
3	0K, par. 1	(initials transcribed without internal spaces)
4	1B1	(statement of responsibility inseparably linked to title proper)
5	1B7	(qualifications retained so as not to abridge title proper before sixth word)
6	1B7	(lengthy author statement preceding chief title abridged after sixth word)
7	1B7	(lengthy title abridged)
8	1C	(parallel title)
9	1G8	(qualifications omitted from statement of responsibility)
10	4B8	(place of publication appears only as part of another area; supplied in modern English form)
11	4C1	(publisher statement includes bookseller)
12	4C2	(address included in publisher statement)
13	4C3	(place of publication transcribed as part of publisher statement)
14	5B3	(pagination sequence includes unnumbered pages)
15	5D1, par. 3	(format)
16	7C1	(nature, scope or artistic form note)
17	7C2	(language of publication note)
18	App. A.1B1	(added entry for chief title)
19	App. A.7C4-5	(added entry for parallel title)

DU SECRET
DES MYSTERES:
OU
L'APOLOGIE
DE LA RUBRIQUE DES MISSELS:
DISSERTATION
THEOLOGIQUE ET HISTORIQUE:

Où l'on montre que :

LA RUBRIQUE DES MISSELS, QUI ORDONNE
de dire fecrètement le Canon de la Meſſe , eſt une con-
tinuation de la Diſcipline du fecret , & du ſilence , que
l'Egliſe Primitive obſervoit , ſur le Myſtère de l'Eucha-
riſtie : Et que

Cette Diſcipline n'ôte point aux Fidèles le moyen d'accom-
pagner le Célébrant , & de s'unir à lui , dans toute la ſuite
du Sacrifice : en quoi conſiſte la meilleure maniere d'en-
tendre la Meſſe.

Par M. P. L. L. DE VALLEMONT, Prêtre,
& Docteur en Théologie.

ΜΥΣΤΙΚΩΣ ΤΑ ΜΥΣΤΙΚΑ:

MYSTERIA MYSTICÈ.

A PARIS,

Chez LE CONTE, & MONTALANT, ſur le Quay
des Auguſtins, à la Ville de Montpellier :
Et chez
La Veûve de JEAN MOREAU, rue Galande, à la
Toiſon d'Or. 1710.

AVEC APROBATION ET PRIVILEGE DU ROY.

SECRET
MYSTERES:
OU
POLOGIE
UBRIQUE DES MISSELS:
ERTATION
IQUE ET HISTORIQUE.

.. DE VALLEMONT, Prêtre,

Docteur en Théologie.

TOME II.

A PARIS,

Chez la Veuve de JEAN MOREAU, ruë
Galande à la Toiſon d'Or. 1710.

AVEC APPROBATION ET PRIVILEGE DU ROY.

EXAMPLE 29: A. Title page to vol. 1 B. Title page to vol. 2, showing variant
publisher statement

EXAMPLE 29

CATALOG RECORD

ref. no.

	100 1	Vallemont, $c abb´e de $q (Pierre Le Lorrain), $d 1649-1721.
1,2,3,4,5,6,7,8	245 10	Du secret des mysteres, ou, L'apologie de la rubrique des missels : $b dissertation theologique et historique ... / $c par M. P.L.L. de Vallemont ...
9,10,11,12,13	260	A Paris : $b Chez Le Conte & Montalant ... `a la ville de Montpellier et chez la ve^uve de Jean Moreau ..., $c 1710.
14,15	300	2 v. ; $c 18 cm. (8vo)
16	500	A criticism of Vert's Explication simple, litt´erale et historique des c´er´emonies de l'Eglise.
17	500	Vol. 2 has variant publisher statement: Chez la ve^uve de Jean Moreau ...
18	500	Initial; head-pieces (1 engraved) and tail-pieces.
19	| LN	Imperfect copy: v. 2, p. 297-298 torn, affecting text.
19	| LN	Bound in 1 v., in full sprinkled calf, gilt-tooled spine, brown leather spine label, red sprinkled edges.
20	740 01	Apologie de la rubrique des missels.
	| 755	Sprinkled calf bindings (Binding) $2 rbbin
	| 755	Sprinkled edges (Binding) $2 rbbin

PRINCIPAL *DCRB* RULES ILLUSTRATED

ref. no.

1	0H, par. 1	(accents not added to "mysteres" or "theologique")
2	0K, par. 1	(initials transcribed without internal spaces)
3	0K, par. 3	(space between two distinct initialisms)
4	1A2, par. 3	(epigram and privilege statement omitted without using mark of omission)
5	1B3	(title proper inclusive of alternative title)
6	1D4	(lengthy other title information abridged)
7	1G7	(title of address in statement of responsibility)
8	1G8	(qualifications omitted from statement of responsibility)
9	4B2	(words or phrases associated with place name transcribed)
10	4B6	(second place of publication recorded as part of publisher statement)
11	4C2	(words or phrases preceding publisher statement transcribed; address omitted)
12	4C6, par. 1	(multiple publishers linked by connecting words; no prescribed punctuation)
13	4C7	(publisher statement of v. 1 transcribed)
14	5B16, par. 3	(issued and bound in different number of volumes)
15	5D1, par. 3	(format)
16	7C1	(nature, scope or artistic form note)
17	7C8	(publication note)
18	7C10	(physical description note)
19	7C18	(copy-specific note)
20	App. A.1B3	(added entry for alternative title)

ANDREÆ TACQUET

Soc. Jesu Matheseos Prof.

ARITHMETICÆ

THEORIA,
ET
PRAXIS

Editio novissima, præcedentibus nitidior,
& emendatior , cui accessit

NICOLAI DE MARTINO

DE PERMUTATIONIBUS,

ET COMBINATIONIBUS

OPVSCVLVM.

NEAPOLI MDCCXXIV.
Ex Typographia Felicis Mosca
Superiorum permissu.

Expensis Bernardini Gessari.

EXAMPLE 30: Title page

EXAMPLE 30

CATALOG RECORD

ref. no.

	100 1	Tacquet, Andr´e, $d 1612-1660.
	240 10	Arithmeticae theoria et praxis
1,2,3	245 10	Andreae Tacquet Soc. Jesu matheseos prof. Arithmeticae theoria, et praxis.
4,5	250	Editio novissima, praecedentibus nitidior, & emendatior / $b cui accessit Nicolai de Martino De permutationibus, et combinationibus opusculum.
6,7,8	260	Neapoli : $b Ex typographia Felicis Mosca : $b Expensis Bernardini Gessari, $c 1724.
9,10,11,12,13	300	[16], 574, [2] p., XII folded leaves of plates : $b ill. (engravings) ; $c 18 cm. (8vo)
14	500	Signatures: a^8 A-2N^8.
15	500	Title vignette; initials.
16	510 4	Backer-Sommervogel, $c VII, column 1810, no. 6
17	500	"Nicolai de Martino De permutationibus, et combinationibus opusculum": p. [531]-574.
	700 12	Martino, Nicol`o di, $d 1701-1769. $t De permutationibus et combinationibus opusculum. $f 1724.
	700 10	Mosca, Felice Carlo, $e printer.
	700 10	Gessari, Bernardino, $e publisher.
18	740 01	Arithmeticae theoria et praxis.
19	740 01	De permutationibus et combinationibus opusculum.

PRINCIPAL *DCRB* RULES ILLUSTRATED

ref. no.

1	0H, par. 2	(transcribe Latin ligature as component letters)
2	1B1	(statement of responsibility inseparably linked to title proper)
3	1G8	(qualifications retained in statement of responsibility)
4	2B1	(words or phrases associated with edition statement transcribed)
5	2C3	(edition statement includes statement of responsibility for a work not necessarily appended to other editions)
6	4C1	(publisher statement includes printer)
7	4C2	(words or phrases preceding publisher statement transcribed)
8	4C6, par. 1	(multiple publisher statements separated by prescribed punctuation)
9	5B1, par. 2	(leaves numbered in roman numerals, transcribed uppercase as they appear)
10	5B3	(pagination sequence includes unnumbered pages)
11	5B10	(folded leaves)
12	5C1	(illustrations; **option**: describe graphic process or technique)
13	5D1, par. 3	(format)
14	7C9	(signatures note)
15	7C10	(physical description note)
16	7C14	(references to published descriptions)
17	7C16	(informal contents note)
18	App. A.1B1	(added entry for chief title)
19	App. A.1E1-2	(added entry for title of additional work)

POEMS

ON

Several Occafions.

By Mr. JOHN GAY.

His jocamur, ludimus, amamus, dolemus, que-
rimur, irafcimur; defcribimus aliquid modò
preffius, modò elatius: atque ipsâ varietate
tentamus efficere, ut alia aliis, quædam
fortaffe omnibus placeant. Plin. Epift.

DUBLIN:

Printed by S. POWELL,

For GEORGE RISK, at *Shakefpear's* Head,
GEORGE EWING, at the *Angel* and *Bible*, and
WILLIAM SMITH, at the *Hercules*, Book-
fellers in *Dame's-ftreet*, MDCCXXIX.

EXAMPLE 31: Title page

EXAMPLE 31

CATALOG RECORD

ref. no.

	100 1	Gay, John, $d 1685-1732.
1,2	245 10	Poems on several occasions / $c by Mr. John Gay.
3,4,5,6	260	Dublin : $b Printed by S. Powell, for George Risk ..., George Ewing ..., and William Smith ..., booksellers ..., $c 1729.
7,8	300	[8], 410, [2] p. ; $c 17 cm. (12mo)
9	500	Signatures: [A]^4 B-L$^{8/4}$ M-Q^{12} R-2G$^{8/4}$ 2H^2.
10	500	Head- and tail-pieces; initials.
11	510 4	ESTC $c t013894
12	500	Subscriber's list: p. [3]-[5] (1st group).
13	500	Advertisements: p. [1]-[2] (3rd group).
12	504	Includes bibliographical references and indexes.
14	505 0	Rural sports -- The fan -- The shepherd's week in six pastorals -- Trivia, or, The art of walking the streets of London -- The what d'ye call it -- Epistles on several occasions -- Tales -- Eclogues -- Miscellanies -- Dione -- Fables.
15	| LN	Half leather, marbled boards, black leather spine label.
15	| LN	From the library of Eliz. Burroughs, with her signature.
	655 7	Occasional poems. $2 rbgenr
	| LAE	Burroughs, Eliz., $e former owner.
	755	Subscription lists (Publishing) $z Ireland $z Dublin $y 1729. $2 rbpub
	| 755	Half bindings (Binding) $2 rbbin
	755	Autographs (Provenance) $x Women $y 18th century. $2 rbprov

PRINCIPAL *DCRB* RULES ILLUSTRATED

ref. no.

1	1A2, par. 3	(epigram omitted without using mark of omission)
2	1G7	(title of address in statement of responsibility)
3	4C1	(publisher statement includes printer and booksellers)
4	4C2	(words or phrases preceding publisher statement transcribed; addresses omitted)
5	4C6, par. 1	(multiple publishers linked by connecting words; no prescribed punctuation)
6	4D2, par. 1	(roman numerals in date transcribed as arabic numerals)
7	5B3	(pagination sequence includes unnumbered pages)
8	5D1, par. 3	(format)
9	7C9	(signatures note)
10	7C10	(physical description note)
11	7C14	(references to published descriptions)
12	7C16	(informal contents note)
13	7C16	(informal contents note: advertisements)
14	7C16	(formal contents note)
15	7C18	(copy-specific note)

AURORA ALEGRE
del dichoso dia de la Gracia
MARIA SANTISSIMA
Digna Madre de Dios.
MES DE VIDA,
donde hallaràn las Almas, pasto
saludable, y dulce para
cada dia.
EPITOME
de los Libros Mystica Ciudad
de Dios, y Vida de la Virgen
Madre de Dios.
Por Fr. Francisco Antonio de
Vereo, Predicador de la Santa
Recoleccion de N.S.P.S. Fran-
cisco de laProvincia del Santo
Evangelio.

CON LICENCIA DE
los Superiores, y privilegio por
diez años del Excmo.Sr. Virrey.
En MEXICO: Por Joseph Ber-
nardo de Hogal, Ministro, ê Im-
pressor del Real Tribunal de la
Santa Cruzada,. Año de 1730.

EXAMPLE 32: Title page to vol. 1

EXAMPLE 32

CATALOG RECORD

ref. no.

	100 1	Vereo, Francisco Antonio de.
1,2,3,4	245 10	Aurora alegre del dichoso dia de la Gracia Maria Santissima digna Madre de Dios : $b mes de vida, donde hallar`an las almas, pasto saludable, y dulce para cada dia : epitome de los libros Mystica ciudad de Dios, y vida de la Virgen Madre de Dios / $c por Fr. Francisco Antonio de Vereo, predicador de la Santa Recoleccion de N.S.P. S. Francisco de la provincia del Santo Evangelio.
5,6,7	260	En Mexico : $b Por Joseph Bernardo de Hogal ..., $c a~no de 1730.
8,9	300	2 v. ([42], 769, [73] p.) : $b 1 ill. ; $c 14 cm. (12mo)
10	500	Based on the M´istica ciudad de Dios of sor Mar´ia de Jes´us de Agreda.
11	500	Title within ornamental border; woodcut on t.p. verso of v. 1: Verdadero retrato de Nuestra Se~nora de Tepepan.
12	510 4	Palau y Dulcet (2nd ed.) $c 360017
13	⎮ LN	Library's copy in old limp vellum, with traces of ties.
	700 01	Mar´ia de Jes´us, $c de Agreda, sor, $d 1602-1665. $t M´istica ciudad de Dios.

PRINCIPAL *DCRB* RULES ILLUSTRATED

ref. no.

1	0H, par. 1	(accents not added to "dia," "Maria," etc.)
2	0K, par. 3	(space between two distinct initialisms)
3	1D2, par. 1	(other titles or phrases following title proper treated as other title information)
4	1G8	(qualifications retained in statement of responsibility)
5	4B2	(words or phrases associated with place name transcribed)
6	4C2	(words or phrases preceding publisher statement transcribed)
7	4D1	(phrase in date transcribed)
8	5D1, par. 3	(format)
9	5B19	(continuous pagination in publication in more than one physical unit)
10	7C1	(nature, scope or artistic form note)
11	7C10	(physical description note)
12	7C14	(references to published descriptions)
13	7C18	(copy-specific note)

A.

RETRAITE
SELON L'ESPRIT
ET LA METHODE
DE
SAINT IGNACE.
NOUVELLE EDITION,
revûë, corrigée & augmentée.

Par le R. P. FRANÇOIS NEPVEU, *de la*
Compagnie de JESUS.

A PARIS,

Chez JEAN-BAPTISTE DELESPINE,
Imprimeur & Libraire ordinaire du Roy,
ruë S. Jacques, à l'Image S. Paul.

M. DCC. XL.
Avec Approbation & Privilege du Roy.

B.

FACE.

& avec réflexion
rés avoir imploré
:l;puis on deman-
n des fautes qu'on
commiſes : enfin
duite ſur l'idée
ans chaque Con-
ectures ſont con-
:s qu'on a medi-
iſes de l'Ecriture,
: Jeſus - Chriſt,
de Rodriguez,
nt les Livres les
& les meilleurs.
quelques - unes
s pour la commo-
i les ont, & quī
bas les autres. J'ai
quatre premiers
:ure , les quatre
iderations de ma
éparer à la mort,
parce qu'elles peuvent être d'un
grand ſecours pour faire une bon-
ne Confeſſion , qui doit être une

á vj

EXAMPLE 33: A. Title page B. Page of text, showing usage of i/j and u/v

EXAMPLE 33

CATALOG RECORD

ref. no.

	100 1	Nepveu, Fran̦cois, $d 1639-1708.
1,2,3,4,5	245 10	Retraite selon l'esprit et la methode de Saint Ignace / $c par le R.P. Fran̦cois Nepveu, de la Compagnie de Jesus.
1,2,6,7	250	Nouvelle edition, revˆuˮe, corrig´ee & augment´ee.
1,2,8,9,10	260	A Paris : $b Chez Jean-Baptiste Delespine ..., $c 1740.
11,12	300	[22], 352 p. ; $c 17 cm. (12mo)
13	500	The author statement appears on the t.p. after the edition statement.
14	500	Signatures: ˜a^{12}(-˜a12) A-O^{12} P^8.
15	500	Initial; head- and tail-pieces.
16	LN	From the library of Robert E. Cushman, with his bookplate.
16	LN	Bound in full sprinkled calf, gilt-tooled spine, red leather spine label, red sprinkled edges, Jesuit seal on front and back covers with lettering: Tolosani Col. Convic.
	655 7	Devotional literature $z France $y 18th century. $2 rbgenr
	700 01	Ignatius, $c of Loyola, Saint, $d 1491-1556. $t Exercitia spiritualia.
	LAE	Cushman, Robert Earl, $e former owner.
	755	Sprinkled calf bindings (Binding) $2 rbbin
	755	Sprinkled edges (Binding) $2 rbbin
	755	Autographs (Provenance) $2 rbprov
	755	Bindings (Provenance) $2 rbprov
	755	Seals (Provenance) $x Jesuit. $2 rbprov

PRINCIPAL *DCRB* RULES ILLUSTRATED

ref. no.

1	0H, par. 1	(accents not added to "methode", "Jesus," "edition," etc.)
2	0H, par. 3	(convert to uppercase or lowercase according to AACR2; transcribe i/j and u/v according to pattern in main text)
3	0K, par. 1	(initials transcribed without internal spaces)
4	1A2, par. 3	(privilege statement omitted without using mark of omission)
5	1G8	(qualifications retained in statement of responsibility)
6	2B1	(words or phrases associated with edition statement transcribed)
7	2C2	(statement of responsibility appears after edition statement)
8	4B2	(words or phrases associated with place name transcribed)
9	4C2	(words or phrases preceding publisher statement transcribed)
10	4D2, par. 1	(roman numerals in date transcribed as arabic numerals)
11	5B3	(pagination sequence includes unnumbered pages)
12	5D1, par. 3	(format)
13	7C6 (4)	(statement of responsibility note: name transposed)
14	7C9	(signatures note)
15	7C10	(physical description note)
16	7C18	(copy-specific note)

ANECDOTES

VENITIENNES
ET
TURQUES
OU
NOUVEAUX MEMOIRES
DU COMTE
DE
BONNEVAL,

*Depuis fon arrivée à Venife jufqu'à fon Exil
dans l'Isle de Chio, au mois de
Mars 1739.*

Par Mr. DE MIRONE.
TOME I.

A LONDRES,
Aux dépens de la Compagnie. 1740.

EXAMPLE 34: Title page to vol. 1

EXAMPLE 34

CATALOG RECORD

ref. no.

	100 2	Lambert de Saumery, Pierre, $d b. ca. 1690.	
1,2,3,4	245 10	Anecdotes venitiennes et turques, ou, Nouveaux memoires du comte de Bonneval : $b depuis son arriv´ee `a Venise jusqu'`a son exil dans l'isle de Chio, au mois de mars 1739 / $c par Mr. de Mirone.	
1,5,6,7	260	A Londres [i.e. Utrecht] : $b Aux d´epens de la Compagnie, $c 1740.	
8,9,10	300	2 v. : $b port. (engraving) ; $c 17 cm. (8vo)	
11	500	By Pierre Lambert de Saumery.	
12	500	Actual place of publication from Weller.	Druckorte.
13	500	Titles in red and black; device on t.p.'s.	
13	500	Head- and tail-pieces; initials.	
14	510 4	Weller, E.O. Falsche Druckorte, $c II, p. 106	
15	LN	Bound in 1 v., in contemporary full leather, blind-ruled covers, gilt-tooled spine and spine label, marbled endpapers, all edges red.	
	655 7	Travel literature. $2 rbgenr	
16	740 01	Nouveaux memoires du comte de Bonneval.	
	755	False imprints (Publishing) $2 rbpub	
	755	Blind tooled bindings (Binding) $2 rbbin	
	755	Marbled papers (Binding) $2 rbbin	
	755	Stained edges (Binding) $2 rbbin	

PRINCIPAL *DCRB* RULES ILLUSTRATED

ref. no.

1	0H, par. 1	(accent not added to "memoires")
2	1A2, par. 4	(volume statement omitted without using mark of omission)
3	1B3	(title proper inclusive of alternative title)
4	1G7	(title of address in statement of responsibility)
5	4B2	(words or phrases associated with place name transcribed)
6	4B9	(fictitious place of publication)
7	4C2	(words or phrases preceding publisher statement transcribed)
8	5B16, par. 3	(issued and bound in different number of volumes)
9	5C1	(illustrations; **option:** describe graphic process or technique)
10	5D1, par. 3	(format)
11	7C6 (1)	(authorship note)
12	7C8	(publication note)
13	7C10	(physical description note)
14	7C14	(reference to published descriptions)
15	7C18	(copy-specific note)
16	App. A.1B3	(added entry for alternative title)

THE

WORKS

OF

Sir *WILLIAM TEMPLE*, Bar^t.

In TWO VOLUMES.

VOLUME *the* FIRST.

To which is prefixed,

The LIFE and CHARACTER of
Sir *WILLIAM TEMPLE*.

Written by a particular FRIEND.

LONDON:

Printed for J. ROUND, R. GOSLING, T. WOODWARD,
S. BIRT, J. and P. KNAPTON, J. CLARK, T. WOTTON,
J. SHUCKBURGH, H. LINTOT, J. and R. TONSON,
C. BATHURST, and M. MEARS.

MDCCXL.

EXAMPLE 35: Title page to vol. 1 (image reduced 35 percent)

EXAMPLE 35

CATALOG RECORD

ref. no.

	100 1	Temple, William, $c Sir, $d 1628-1699.
	240 10	Works. $f 1740
1,2,3,4	245 14	The works of Sir William Temple, bart. : $b in two volumes ... : to which is prefixed, The life and character of Sir William Temple, written by a particular friend.
5,6,7	260	London : $b Printed for J. Round ... [and 11 others], $c 1740.
8	300	2 v. ; $c 36 cm. (fol.)
9	500	Each work has special title page.
9	500	Engraved frontispiece to vol. 1 (portrait of Sir William Temple by G. Vertue after Lely).
10	510 4	ESTC $c t145994
11	505 0	v. 1. The life and character of Sir William Temple / written by a particular friend [his sister, Lady Martha Giffard] Observations upon the United Provinces of the Netherlands. Miscellanea. Memoirs, the third part, from the peace concluded 1679 to the time of the author's retirement from publick business. Memoirs of what past in Christendom from the war begun 1672, to the peace concluded 1679 -- v. 2. Letters written by Sir William Temple, bart., and other ministers of state ... from 1665 to 1672 ... / pub. by Jonathan Swift. Letters to the king ... and other persons ... / pub. by Jonathan Swift. An introduction to the history of England.
12	LN	Library's copy in old panelled calf, with binder's title: Temple's works; ink inscription ("Charles Steyning, Highden, May 6th 1792") on front fly-leaf of vol. 1.
	700 10	Swift, Jonathan, $d 1667-1745.
	700 12	Giffard, Martha, $c Lady, $d 1638-1722. $t Life and character of Sir William Temple, bart. $f 1740.
	LAE	Steyning, Charles, $e former owner.
13	LTE	Temple's works.

PRINCIPAL *DCRB* RULES ILLUSTRATED

ref. no.

1	1A1, par. 4	(colon precedes each unit of other title information)
2	1B1	(statement of responsibility inseparably linked to title proper)
3	1D3	(volume/part designation transcribed as other title information)
4	1D2, par. 2	(other title information constitutes formal statement of contents)
5	4C2	(words or phrases preceding publisher statement transcribed)
6	4C6, par. 1	(multiple publisher statements; first statement plus [and *x* others])
7	4D2, par. 1	(roman numerals in date transcribed as arabic numerals)
8	5D1, par. 3	(format)
9	7C10	(physical description note)
10	7C14	(references to published descriptions)
11	7C16	(formal contents (from t.p.) note)
12	7C18	(copy-specific note)
13	App. A.7C18	(added entry for copy-specific title: binder's title)

T. LUCRETIUS CARUS

OF THE

NATURE of *THINGS,*

IN SIX BOOKS.

ILLUSTRATED with

Proper and Useful NOTES.

Adorned with COPPER-PLATES,

Curiously ENGRAVED

By *GUERNIER*, and others.

Carmina fublimis *tunc funt peritura* Lucretî
Exitio Terras cum dabit una Dies. OVID.

IN TWO VOLUMES.

LONDON:
Printed for DANIEL BROWNE, at the *Black Swan*
without *Temple-Bar.*
MDCCXLIII

EXAMPLE 36: Title page to vol. 1

EXAMPLE 36

CATALOG RECORD

ref. no.

	100 2	Lucretius Carus, Titus.
	240 10	De rerum natura. $l English & Latin
1,2,3,4,5,6,7	245 10	Of the nature of things : $b in six books / $c T. Lucretius Carus ; illustrated with proper and useful notes ; adorned with copper-plates, curiously engraved by Guernier, and others ; in two volumes.
8,9	260	London : $b Printed for Daniel Browne ..., $c 1743.
10	300	2 v. : $b ill. ; $c 21 cm. (8vo)
11	500	Translation of: De rerum natura.
12	500	Latin text and English prose translation on opposite pages.
13	500	Author's name transposed from head of title.
14	500	Illustrations on folded leaves of plates.
15	510 4	ESTC $c t049793
15	510 4	Gordon, C.A. Lucretius, $c 502B
16	500	Includes indexes.
17 |	LN	From the library of Chester Noyes Greenough and Ruth Hornblower Greenough, with their bookplates.
	700 10	Du Guernier, Louis, $d 1677-1716, $e engraver.
|	LAE	Greenough, Chester Noyes, $d 1874-1938, $e former owner.
|	LAE	Greenough, Ruth Hornblower, $e former owner.
	700 10	Browne, Daniel, $e bookseller.
18	740 01	T. Lucretius Carus Of the nature of things.
|	755	Bookplates (Provenance) $2 rbprov

PRINCIPAL *DCRB* RULES ILLUSTRATED

ref. no.

1	1A2, par. 3	(epigram omitted without using mark of omission)
2	1B1	(statement of responsibility separable from title proper; transposed to appropriate area of record)
3	1D3	(volume/part designation transcribed as other title information)
4	1G3	(statement of responsibility transposed without using mark of omission)
5	1G6	(multiple statements of responsibility)
6	1G12	(statement of responsibility without explicitly named person or body)
7	1G14, par. 2	(phrase transcribed after statement of responsibility; punctuated as subsequent statement of responsibility)
8	4C2	(words or phrases preceding publisher statement transcribed; address omitted)
9	4D2, par. 1	(roman numerals in date transcribed as arabic numerals)
10	5D1, par. 3	(format)
11	7C2	(language of publication note; translation)
12	7C2	(language of publication note)
13	7C6 (4)	(statement of responsibility note: name transposed)
14	7C10	(physical description note)
15	7C14	(references to published descriptions)
16	7C16	(informal contents note)
17	7C18	(copy-specific note)
18	App. A.1B1	(added entry for title proper)

Stultus verſus *Sapientem* :

IN THREE

LETTERS

TO THE

FOOL,

ON

SUBJECTS the moſt Intereſting.

By HENRY FIELDING, Eſq;

Joculare tibi videtur : & ſane lœve,
Dum nihil habemus majus, calamo ludimus.
Sed diligenter intuere has nœnias ;
Quantum jubillis utilitatem reperies !

PHÆD.

LONDON: Printed and
DUBLIN Re-printed by E. BATE, in
Gorge's-Lane, 1749.

EXAMPLE 37: Title page

EXAMPLE 37

CATALOG RECORD

ref. no.

	100	1	Fielding, Henry, $d 1707-1754.
1,2	245	10	Stultus versus Sapientem : $b in three letters to the fool, on subjects the most interesting / $c by Henry Fielding, Esq.
3,4,5,6	260		[Dublin] : $b London printed and Dublin re-printed by E. Bate, in George's-Lane, $c 1749.
7,8,9	300		23, [1] p. (the last p. blank) ; $c 17 cm. (8vo)
10	510	4	ESTC $c n024312
11		LN	From the library of Jerome Kern, with his bookplate.
	655	7	Letters. $2 rbgenr
	655	7	Satires. $2 rbgenr
		LAE	Kern, Jerome, $d 1885-1945, $e former owner.
		755	Bookplates (Provenance) $2 rbprov

PRINCIPAL *DCRB* RULES ILLUSTRATED

ref. no.

1	1A2, par. 3	(epigram omitted without using mark of omission)
2	1G7	(title of address in statement of responsibility transcribed)
3	4B8	(place of publication appears only as part of another area; supplied in modern English form)
4	4C1	(publisher statement includes printer)
5	4C2	(words or phrases preceding publisher statement transcribed; address included)
6	4C3	(place of publication transcribed as part of publisher statement)
7	5B3	(pagination sequence includes unnumbered pages)
8	5B7, par. 1	(expansion of statement of extent)
9	5D1, par. 3	(format)
10	7C14	(references to published descriptions)
11	7C18	(copy-specific note)

CONSTANTIA;

OR, A

TRUE PICTURE

OF

HUMAN LIFE,

Reprefented in

Fifteen Evening Converfations,

After the Manner of BOCCACE.

In TWO VOLUMES.

To which is prefixed,

A Short DISCOURSE on Novel Writing.

LONDON:

Printed for A. MILLAR, over-againft Catharine-ftreet
in the Strand. M,DCC,LI.

EXAMPLE 38: Title page to vol. I

EXAMPLE 38

CATALOG RECORD

ref. no.

1,2,3	245 00	Constantia, or, A true picture of human life : $b represented in fifteen evening conversations, after the manner of Boccace : in two volumes : to which is prefixed, A short discourse on novel writing.
4,5	260	London : $b Printed for A. Millar ..., $c 1751.
6,7	300	2 v. ; $c 17 cm. (12mo)
8	500	Head-pieces; initials; press figures.
9	510 4	ESTC $c n005136
10	LN	Bound in gilt-ruled, full sprinkled calf, gilt-tooled red morocco spine labels, red sprinkled edges.
	655 7	Imaginary conversations $y 18th century. $2 rbgenr
12	730 02	Short discourse on novel writing. $f 1751.
11	740 01	Constantia.
11	740 01	True picture of human life.
	755	Press figures (Printing) $2 rbpri
	755	Sprinkled calf bindings (Binding) $2 rbbin
	755	Sprinkled edges (Binding) $2 rbbin

PRINCIPAL *DCRB* RULES ILLUSTRATED

ref. no.

1	1B3	(title proper inclusive of alternative title)
2	1D2, par. 1	(other titles or phrases following title proper treated as other title information)
3	1D3	(volume/part designation transcribed as other title information)
4	4C2	(words or phrases preceding publisher statement transcribed; address omitted)
5	4D2, par. 1	(roman numerals in date transcribed as arabic numerals)
6	5B16	(publication in more than one physical unit)
7	5D1, par.3	(format)
8	7C10	(physical description note)
9	7C14	(references to published descriptions)
10	7C18	(copy-specific note)
11	App. A.1B3	(added entry for alternative title)
12	App. A.1E1-2	(added entry for title of additional work)

Caraccioli, L. A.

LE
LIVRE
DE QUATRE
COULEURS.

Ridenda  dicere

verum   quid vetat?

AUX QUATRE-ÉLÉMENTS,

De l'Imprimerie des QUATRE-SAISONS.

4444.

EXAMPLE 39: Title page

EXAMPLE 39

CATALOG RECORD

ref. no.

	100 1	Caraccioli, Louis-Antoine, $c marquis, $d 1719-1803.
1	245 13	Le livre de quatre couleurs.
2	260	Aux Quatre-´El´ements : $b De l'imprimerie des quatre-saisons, $c 4444 $a [i.e. Paris : $b Duchesne, $c 1760]
3,4	300	[4], xxiv, 110 p. ; $c 17 cm. (8vo)
5	500	By Louis-Antoine Caraccioli; author and actual imprint supplied from Barbier.
7	500	The text is dated at end "A Paris, ce 3 ao^ut, 1757" and reference sources vary in supplying date, cf. below.
6	500	NUC pre-1956 cites eds. of 110 and 114 p.
8	500	Signatures: pi^2 A-H^8/^{4} I-K^8 L^4(-L4, blank).
9	500	Printed in green, brown, red and yellow-orange.
10	510 4	Barbier, A.A. Ouvrages anonymes, $c II, column 1327
10	510 4	Brunet, $c III, column 1122
10	510 4	Cioranescu, A. 18. s., $c 15478
10	510 4	Gr¨asse, $c II, p. 44
11	LN	Library stamp on t.p. cancelled with black ink.
11	LN	Ms. bibliographical notice (from Brunet) pasted to front endpaper.
11	LN	Bound in paste-paper boards with calf shelfback, hinges broken, spine detached and broken.
	755	Fictitious imprints (Publishing) $z France $y 18th century. $2 rbpub
	755	Printing in multiple colors (Printing) $z France $y 18th century. $2 rbpri

PRINCIPAL *DCRB* RULES ILLUSTRATED

ref. no.

1	1A2, par. 3	(motto omitted without using mark of omission)
2	4A4	(fictitious imprint; correct imprint supplied from reference source)
3	5B3	(pagination sequence includes unnumbered pages)
4	5D1, par. 3	(format)
5	7C6 (1)	(authorship note; source of attribution included)
6	7C7	(edition and bibliographic history note)
7	7C8	(publication note)
8	7C9	(signatures note)
9	7C10	(physical description note)
10	7C14	(references to published descriptions)
11	7C18	(copy-specific note)

Divine Miscellanies;

OR, SACRED

POEMS.

IN TWO PARTS.

PART I. Sacred to Christian Devotion and Piety,

CONSISTING OF

HYMNS and DIVINE MEDITATIONS,

Upon various Subjects and Occasions
Chiefly from the AUTHOR's own Experience.

PART II. Sacred to practical Virtue and Holiness,
Containing three EPISTLES.

I. A practical PARAPHRASE on the TEN COMMANDMENTS.

Humbly address'd to the Church of England, upon their excellent
Order of Reading them.

II. The CHRISTIAN WARFARE;

Or, a serious Exhortation to Virtue and Piety:

Humbly address'd to the Protestant Dissenters.

III. The Divine Original and primitive Beauty of CHRISTIANITY.

Set-forth in the Birth, Life, Sufferings, Death, Resurrection and
Ascension of our LORD and SAVIOUR

JESUS CHRIST,

And the Life and Conduct of his APOSTLES:

Humbly address'd to all Professors of Christianity, for their holy
Imitation. Written in plain and easy Language,

For the Delight and Improvement of all Lovers
of DIVINE POETRY;

By JAMES MAXWELL.

COLL. iii. 16.----Teaching and admonishing one another in
Psalms and Hymns, and spiritual Songs, singing with Grace in
your Hearts to the Lord.

✝✝✝✝✝✝✝✝✝✝✝✝✝✝✝✝✝✝✝✝✝✝✝✝✝✝✝✝✝✝✝✝✝✝✝

BIRMINGHAM: Printed for the AUTHOR,
by T. WARREN, jun. MDCCLVI.

EXAMPLE 40A: Title page

EXAMPLE 40A

CATALOG RECORD

ref. no.

	100 1	Maxwell, James, $d 1720-1800.
1,2,3,4,5	245 10	Divine miscellanies, or, Sacred poems : $b in two parts ... : written in plain and easy language, for the delight and improvement of all lovers of divine poetry / $c by James Maxwell.
1,6,7	260	Birmingham : $b Printed for the author, by T. Warren, Jun., $c 1756.
8,9	300	[28], 324 p., [1] leaf of plates : $b ill. ; $c 17 cm. (12mo)
10	500	Signatures: A^{12} a^2 B-2E^6.
11	500	Initials; head- and tail-pieces.
12	500	List of subscribers: p. [3]-[11] (1st group).
13	500	Errata: p. [28] (1st group).
11	504	Includes bibliographical references.
14	505 0	(from t.p.) Part I. Sacred to Christian devotion and piety, consisting of hymns and divine meditations ... -- Part II. Sacred to practical virtue and holiness, containing three epistles. I. A practical paraphrase on the Ten Commandments ... II. The Christian warfare ... III. The divine original and primitive beauty of Christianity ...
	655 7	Devotional literature. $2 rbgenr
15	740 01	Divine miscellanies.
15	740 01	Sacred poems.
	755	Errata lists (Printing) $2 rbpri
	755	Subscription lists (Publishing) $z England $z Birmingham $y 18th century. $2 rbpub

PRINCIPAL *DCRB* RULES ILLUSTRATED

ref. no.

1	0H, par. 3	(convert to uppercase or lowercase according to AACR2)
2	1A2, par. 3	(bible verse omitted without using mark of omission)
3	1B3	(title proper inclusive of alternative title)
4	1D2, par. 2	(other title information constitutes formal statement of contents)
5	1D3	(volume/part designation transcribed as other title information)
6	4C2	(words or phrases preceding publisher statement transcribed)
7	4D2, par. 1	(roman numerals in date transcribed as arabic numerals)
8	5B3	(pagination sequence includes unnumbered pages)
9	5D1, par. 3	(format)
10	7C9	(signatures note)
11	7C10	(physical description note)
12	7C16	(informal contents note)
13	7C16	(informal contents note: mandatory errata leaf note)
14	7C16	(formal contents (from t.p.) note)
15	App. A.1B3	(added entry for alternative title)

Divine Miscellanies;
OR, SACRED
POEMS.
IN TWO PARTS.

PART I. Sacred to Christian Devotion and Piety,
CONSISTING OF

HYMNS and DIVINE MEDITATIONS,
Upon various Subjects and Occasions
Chiefly from the AUTHOR's own Experience.

PART II. Sacred to practical Virtue and Holiness,
Containing three EPISTLES.

I. A practical PARAPHRASE on the
TEN COMMANDMENTS.

Humbly address'd to the Church of England, upon their excellent
Order of Reading them.

II. The CHRISTIAN WARFARE;
Or, a serious Exhortation to Virtue and Piety:

Humbly address'd to the Protestant Dissenters.

III. The Divine Original and primitive
Beauty of CHRISTIANITY.

Set-forth in the Birth, Life, Sufferings, Death, Resurrection and
Ascension of our LORD and SAVIOUR

JESUS CHRIST,

And the Life and Conduct of his APOSTLES:

Humbly address'd to all Professors of Christianity, for their holy
Imitation. Written in plain and easy Language,

For the Delight and Improvement of all Lovers
of DIVINE POETRY;

By JAMES MAXWELL.

COLL. iii. 16.----Teaching and admonishing one another in
Psalms and Hymns, and spiritual Songs, singing with Grace in
your Hearts to the Lord.

✠✠✠✠✠✠✠✠✠✠✠✠✠✠✠✠-✠✠✠✠✠✠✠✠✠✠✠✠✠✠✠✠

BIRMINGHAM: Printed for the AUTHOR,
by T. WARREN, jun. MDCCLVI.

EXAMPLE 40B: Title page

EXAMPLE 40B

MINIMAL-LEVEL CATALOG RECORD, WITHOUT OPTIONS

ref. no.

	100 1	Maxwell, James, $d 1720-1800.
1,2,3,4,5,10	245 10	Divine miscellanies, or, Sacred poems : $b in two parts ... / $c by James Maxwell.
6,7	260	Birmingham : $b Printed for the author, by T. Warren, Jun., $c 1756.
8,9	300	[28], 324 p., [1] leaf of plates : $b ill. ; $c 17 cm. (12mo)

PRINCIPAL *DCRB* RULES ILLUSTRATED

ref. no.

1	0H, par. 3	(convert to uppercase or lowercase according to AACR2)
2	1A2, par. 3	(bible verse omitted without using mark of omission)
3	1B3	(title proper inclusive of alternative title)
4	1D3	(volume/part designation transcribed as other title information)
5	1D4	(lengthy other title information abridged)
6	4C2	(words or phrases preceding publisher statement transcribed)
7	4D2, par. 1	(roman numerals in date transcribed as arabic numerals)
8	5B3	(pagination sequence includes unnumbered pages)
9	5D1, par. 3	(format)
10	App. D	(minimal-level record, without options; areas 0-6 and 8 followed, all allowable abridgements made, no mandatory notes made, no notes in area 7 made, title and special files access points omitted)

Divine Miſcellanies;
OR, SACRED
POEMS.
IN TWO PARTS.

PART I. Sacred to Chriſtian Devotion and Piety,
CONSISTING OF

HYMNS and DIVINE MEDITATIONS,

Upon various Subjects and Occaſions
Chiefly from the AUTHOR's own Experience.

PART II. Sacred to practical Virtue and Holineſs,
Containing three EPISTLES.

I. A practical PARAPHRASE on the
TEN COMMANDMENTS.

Humbly addreſs'd to the Church of England, upon their excellent
Order of Reading them.

II. The CHRISTIAN WARFARE;

Or, a ſerious Exhortation to Virtue and Piety:

Humbly addreſs'd to the Proteſtant Diſſenters.

III. The Divine Original and primitive
Beauty of CHRISTIANITY.

Set-forth in the Birth, Life, Sufferings, Death, Reſurrection and
Aſcenſion of our LORD and SAVIOUR

JESUS CHRIST,

And the Life and Conduct of his APOSTLES:

Humbly addreſs'd to all Profeſſors of Chriſtianity, for their holy
Imitation. Written in plain and eaſy Language,

For the Delight and Improvement of all Lovers
of DIVINE POETRY;

By JAMES MAXWELL.

COLL. iii. 16.----Teaching and admoniſhing one another in
Pſalms and Hymns, and ſpiritual Songs, ſinging with Grace in
your Hearts to the Lord.

✠✠✠✠✠✠✠✠✠✠✠✠✠✠✠✠✠✠✠✠✠✠✠✠✠✠✠✠✠✠✠✠✠✠✠✠✠

BIRMINGHAM: Printed for the AUTHOR,
by T. WARREN, jun. MDCCLVI.

EXAMPLE 40C: Title page

EXAMPLE 40C

MINIMAL-LEVEL CATALOG RECORD, WITH OPTIONS

ref. no.

	100	1	Maxwell, James, $d 1720-1800.
1,2,3,4,5,12	245	10	Divine miscellanies, or, Sacred poems : $b in two parts ... / $c by James Maxwell.
6,7	260		Birmingham : $b Printed for the author, by T. Warren, Jun., $c 1756.
8,9	300		[28], 324 p., [1] leaf of plates : $b ill. ; $c 17 cm. (12mo)
10	500		Errata: p. [28] (1st group).
	655	7	Devotional literature. $2 rbgenr
11	740	01	Divine miscellanies.
11	740	01	Sacred poems.
	755		Errata lists (Printing) $2 rbpri
	755		Subscription lists (Publishing) $z England $z Birmingham $y 18th century. $2 rbpub

PRINCIPAL *DCRB* RULES ILLUSTRATED

ref. no.

1	0H, par. 3	(convert to uppercase or lowercase according to AACR2)
2	1A2, par. 3	(bible verse omitted without using mark of omission)
3	1B3	(title proper inclusive of alternative title)
4	1D3	(volume/part designation transcribed as other title information)
5	1D4	(lengthy other title information abridged)
6	4C2	(words or phrases preceding publisher statement transcribed)
7	4D2, par. 1	(roman numerals in date transcribed as arabic numerals)
8	5B3	(pagination sequence includes unnumbered pages)
9	5D1, par. 3	(format)
10	7C16	(informal contents note: mandatory errata leaf note)
11	App. A.1B3	(added entry for alternative title)
12	App. D	(minimal-level record, with options; areas 0-6 and 8 followed, all allowable abridgements made, mandatory notes made, no notes in area 7 made, title and special files access points made)

THOUGHTS

CONCERNING

BANKS and the PAPER-CURRENCY

OF

SCOTLAND.

BANKS and paper-money have very defervedly become the objects of general attention in Scotland. Their operations have been fo greatly extended, they have produced fuch remarkable changes upon the methods of circulation, the means of obtaining and fupporting credit, the courfe of exchange, and indeed upon the whole of our money dealings, that their effects can be no longer indifferent; they muft either have proved beneficial or detrimental to the public intereft.

It appears, that if paper-money can be made to ferve all the purpofes of real money, and can at all times readily command it, that it muft be of advantage to any country, even tho' it fhould not be current any where elfe. Let us fuppofe the gold and filver, neceffary for the circulation of a nation, to be four millions, and that paper may be fubftituted in the place of one half of that fum; this would enable that nation to pay off two millions of debt, or to lend two millions to other countries, or to employ them ftill more profitably, by promoting induftry, in all its various branches, of agriculture, manufactures, and trade. Thus, at leaft, the intereft of two millions muft be gained by the introduction of that paper-money, which would anfwer all the ends that gold and filver formerly did, if it be allowed that the fpecie remaining is a fufficient fund, at all times, for the bank, or bankers, to pay for any part of the paper that may be demanded of them.

The truth of this reafoning is further confirmed, by the experience and practice of all the great commercial kingdoms and ftates in Europe, that enjoy the fecurity of a free government. There banks and bankers have fubfifted for many ages, trade has flourifhed by their influence, and kept pace with their increafe. Arbitrary governments indeed, are deftructive of that truft and confidence upon which a bank alone depends.

The credit of the Bank of England, founded on real wealth, and fupported by prompt payments, has long ftood unfhaken, even in the moft difficult and trying times. This bank has afforded fuch aids, both to public and private credit, as might feem incredible to thofe who have not had accefs to know, not only the great loans advanced to the government, but alfo the immenfe fums it difcounts on private bills, for the conveniency of foreign as well as Britifh commerce. It keeps the cafh of merchants, whofe orders are punctually anfwered, to the extent of the money they have lodged. It iffues bills or promiffory notes, which are always readily paid when demanded. The private bankers, in different parts of London, and in the principal trading towns in England, carry on bufinefs in the fame manner as the Bank: They difcount bills to a very large extent; they keep the cafh of landed men, merchants, and manufacturers; and they iffue bills and promiffory notes, which, upon demand, regularly find payment in fpecie. The great utility of this whole clafs of dealers in England, is univerfally felt and acknowledged. The Bank of England, tho' incorporated by act of Parliament, has no exclufive privilege of iffuing bills or notes, nor pretends to any; it allows the private bankers, undifturbed, to follow the fame branches of bufinefs with itfelf, without thinking of procuring any law to reftrain them in the extent of their bufinefs, or of the fums to be inferted in their notes; it employs no open or concealed agents, in different corners, to pick up the notes of private bankers from the circulation, in order to introduce its own; far

EXAMPLE 41: First page of text (image reduced 40 percent)

EXAMPLE 41

CATALOG RECORD

ref. no.

		245 00	Thoughts concerning banks and the paper-currency of Scotland.
1,2		260	[Scotland : $b s.n.], $c 1763.
3,4		300	3, [1] p. ; $c 39 cm. (fol.)
5		500	Caption title.
6		500	At head of title: November, 1763.
7		510 4	Kress Lib., $c 6144
8	|	LN	Disbound, previously folded in smaller binding, bottom third of inner margin cut away at fold.

PRINCIPAL *DCRB* RULES ILLUSTRATED

ref. no.

1	4B12	(probable place of publication supplied from reference source)
2	4C9	(publisher unknown)
3	5B2	(statement of extent for a normally imposed single sheet given in same manner as for a volume)
4	5D1, par. 3	(format)
5	7C3	(source of title proper note)
6	7C8	(publication note)
7	7C14	(references to published descriptions)
8	7C18	(copy-specific note)

Expofition Succincte

de

l'Origine et des Progrès

du Peuple qu'on appelle

les QUAKERS ou les TREMBLEURS :

Où l'on declare ingenûment leur Principe Fondamental, leurs Doctrines, leur Culte, leur Miniftère, et leur Difcipline.

Avec un Abregé des précedentes Œconomies ou Difpenfations de Dieu au Monde, par voie d'Introduction.

Par GUILLAUME PENN.

A quoi l'on a ajouté un des Temoignages rendus à la Lumiére, par GEORGE FOX.

Le Tout traduit de l'*Anglois* par CLAUDE GAY.

Comme inconnus : Et toutefois étant reconnus. 2 *Cor*. vi. 9.

Mais Il étoit envoyé pour rendre Temoignage à la Lumiére. Cette Lumiére étoit la veritable, qui illumine tout homme venant au Monde. *Jean* i. 8, 9.

A LONDRES :

Imprimé par Luc Hinde demeurant dans *George-yard en Lombard-ftreet*. 1764.

EXAMPLE 42: Title page

EXAMPLE 42

CATALOG RECORD

ref. no.

	100 1	Penn, William, $d 1644-1718.
	240 10	Brief account of the rise and progress of the people called Quakers. $l French
1,2,3,4,5,6,7	245 10	Exposition succincte de l'origine et des progr`es du peuple qu'on appelle les quakers ou les trembleurs : $b o^u l'on declare ingen^ument leur principe fondamental, leurs doctrines, leur culte, leur minist`ere, et leur discipline : avec un abreg´e des pr´ecedentes @conomies ou dispensations de Dieu au monde, par voie d'introduction / $c par Guillaume Penn ; a quoi l'on a ajout´e un des temoignages rendus `a la lumi`ere, par George Fox ; le tout traduit de l'anglois par Claude Gay.
1,8,9,10	260	A Londres : $b Imprim´e par Luc Hinde ..., $c 1764.
11,12,13	300	iv, 109, [3] p. ; $c 20 cm. (8vo)
14	500	Translation of: A brief account of the rise and progress of the people called Quakers.
15	500	Signatures: A-O^4 P^2.
16	500	"Instruction pour tous ceux qui voudront conno^itre le chemin du royaume [par] George Fox": p. [89]-109.
17	500	Errata: p. [2] (3rd group).
18	LN	Quarter bound in marbled boards, red sprinkled edges.
	700 10	Gay, Claude, $d 1707?-1786, $e tr.
	700 12	Fox, George, $d 1624-1691. $t To all that would know the way to the kingdom. $l French. $f 1764.
	700 10	Hinde, Luke, $d fl. 1750-1767, $e printer.
19	740 01	Instruction pour tous ceux qui voudront conno^itre le chemin du royaume.
	755	Quarter bindings (Binding) $2 rbbin
	755	Sprinkled edges (Binding) $2 rbbin

PRINCIPAL *DCRB* RULES ILLUSTRATED

ref. no.

1	0H, par. 1	(accents not added to "declare," "temoignages," etc.)
2	0H, par. 2	(transcribe French ligature as single character)
3	1A1, par. 4	(colon precedes each unit of other title information)
4	1A2, par. 3	(epigram omitted without using mark of omission)
5	1D2, par. 1	(other titles or phrases following title proper treated as other title information)
6	1G6	(multiple statements of responsibility)
7	1G14, par. 2	(phrase transcribed after statement of responsibility; punctuated as subsequent statement of responsibility)
8	4B1	(place of publication transcribed as it appears)
9	4B2	(words or phrases associated with place name transcribed)
10	4C2	(words or phrases preceding publisher statement transcribed; address omitted)
11	5B3	(pagination sequence includes unnumbered pages)
12	5B4	(errata leaf included in statement of extent)
13	5D1, par. 3	(format)
14	7C2	(language of publication note; translation)
15	7C9	(signatures note)
16	7C16	(informal contents note)
17	7C16	(informal contents note: mandatory errata leaf note)
18	7C18	(copy-specific note)
19	App. A.1E1-2	(added entry for title of additional work)

GEOGRAPHY

Made familiar and easy to

Young Gentlemen and Ladies,

BEING THE

SIXTH VOLUME

OF THE

Circle of the Sciences, &c.

Publifhed by the KING's *Authority.*

The FOURTH EDITION.

LONDON:

Printed for T. CARNAN, and F. NEWBERY,
Junior, at No. 65, St. Paul's Church-
Yard.

M.DCC.LXXVI.

EXAMPLE 43: Title page

EXAMPLE 43

CATALOG RECORD

ref. no.

1	245 00	Geography made familiar and easy to young gentlemen and ladies : $b being the sixth volume of The Circle of the sciences, &c. / $c published by the King's authority.
2	250	The fourth edition.
3,4	260	London : $b Printed for T. Carnan, and F. Newbery, Junior ..., $c 1776.
5,6	300	[20], 319, [13] p. ; $c 11 cm. (32mo in 8s)
8	500	Edited by John Newbery. Cf. Osborne Coll., I, p. 133.
9	500	First published in 1748 by John Newbery. Cf. NUC pre-1956 416:653.
10	500	Signatures: A-Y^8.
11	500	Roscoe records no definite information on the presence of a folding map, which is present in the first ed. No copies of the fourth ed. with a map are recorded.
13	500	Integral publisher's ads: [13] p. at end.
12	510 4	ESTC $c t112043
12	510 4	Roscoe, S. John Newbery, $c J63(4)
14	| LN	From the library of Elisabeth Ball.
14	| LN	Bound in original blue boards, damaged, with green vellum shelfback; printed paper label on spine.
	700 10	Newbery, John, $d 1713-1767.
	| LAE	Ball, Elisabeth, $d 1897-1982, $e former owner.
7	830 0	Circle of the sciences ; $v v. 6.

PRINCIPAL *DCRB* RULES ILLUSTRATED

ref. no.

1	1G12	(statement of responsibility without explicitly named person or body)
2	2B1	(words or phrases associated with edition statement transcribed)
3	4C2	(words or phrases preceding publisher statement transcribed; address omitted)
4	4D2, par. 1	(roman numerals in date transcribed as arabic numerals)
5	5B3	(pagination sequence includes unnumbered pages)
6	5D1, par. 3	(format)
7	6	(series in pre-1801 work)
8	7C6 (1)	(authorship note; source of attribution included)
9	7C7	(edition and bibliographic history note)
10	7C9	(signatures note)
11	7C10	(physical description note)
12	7C14	(references to published descriptions)
13	7C16	(informal contents note; advertisements)
14	7C18	(copy-specific note)

N°. 26.

LES SABATS

JACOBITES.

Inutilité et danger des Clubs.

Le mal est fait, il faut se résigner et le sup-
porter: que ne puis-je dire y porter remède !
Je le dirois peut-être si ces assemblées d'hommes,
que des circonstances difficiles ont fait naître,
n'étoient pas devenues le foyer de la licence.
A l'aurore de la liberté, quand la constitution
n'existoit pas, il étoit naturel que chacun s'occu-
pât du sort qu'il pouvoit espérer, des dangers
qu'il avoit à redouter, des vertus qu'il devoit
acquérir et des loix qu'il faudroit observer; il
n'etoit pas étonnant que chacun voulût s'en
entretenir, et puiser dans le commerce de ses
semblables les lumières et la patience.

Aujourd'hui la constitution est faite, le sort
de tous les habitans de la France est à-peu-près
fixé: ceux, qui sont encore dans l'incertitude

A 2

EXAMPLE 44: Page 3 of issue no. 26

EXAMPLE 44

CATALOG RECORD

ref. no.

	100	1	Marchant, Fran,cois, $d 1761-1793.
	245	14	Les sabats jacobites.
1	260		[Paris] : $b J. Blanchon, $c -1792.
2	300		3 v. : $b ill. ; $c 22 cm. (8vo)
	362	1	Began in 1791.
	362	0	-no 75.
3	500		Description based on: No 26; title from caption.
4	500		By Fran,cois Marchant. Cf. NUC pre-1956 513:105.
5	500		Place of publication from publisher-supplied volume t.p.
	515		No 26-no 50 called t. 2; no 51-no 75 called t. 3e.
6	510	4	Martin & Walter. Cat. de la R´evolution fran,caise, $c V, p. 1306
7	|	LN	Bound in blue pasteboard, edges untrimmed.
8	|	LN	Bound with v. 3 is the author's Les grands sabats, pour servir de suite aux Sabats jacobites.
	|	755	Pasteboard (Binding) $2 rbbin
	785	00	Marchant, Fran,cois, $d 1761-1793. $t Grands sabats, pour servir de suite aux Sabats jacobites $w (OCoLC) 10461385 $w (DLC)sc 84008709

PRINCIPAL *DCRB* RULES ILLUSTRATED

ref. no.

1	App. C.1.4	(rare serials: information supplied from source other than prescribed source of information)
2	5D1, par. 3	(format)
3	7C3	(source of title proper note)
4	7C6 (1)	(authorship note; source of attribution included)
5	7C8	(publication note)
6	7C14	(references to published descriptions)
7	7C18	(copy-specific note)
8	7C19	(copy-specific "with:" note)

LA
RÉVOLUTION FRANÇOISE
A
GENÈVE;

TABLEAU
HISTORIQUE ET POLITIQUE
DE
LA CONDUITE DE LA FRANCE
ENVERS LES GENEVOIS,

DEPUIS LE MOIS D'OCTOBRE 1792, AU MOIS D'OCTOBRE
1794

Veluti in Speculo.

LONDRES:

De l'Imprimerie de T. SPILSBURY & FILS.

Se vend chez P. ELMSLEY, *Strand;* J. DEBRETT,
Piccadilly; & J. DE BOFFE, *Gerrard-Street, Soho.*

EXAMPLE 45: Title page

EXAMPLE 45

CATALOG RECORD

ref. no.

	100 1	Ivernois, Francis d', $c Sir, $d 1757-1842.
1	245 13	La R´evolution fran.coise a Gen`eve : $b tableau historique et politique de la conduite de la France envers les genevois, depuis le mois d'octobre 1792, au mois d'octobre 1794.
2,3,4,5,6	260	Londres : $b De l'imprimerie de T. Spilsbury & fils : $b Se vend chez P. Elmsley ..., J. Debrett ..., & J. De Boffe ..., $c [1794 or 1795]
7	300	75, [1] p. ; $c 22 cm.
8	500	Written by Francis d'Ivernois. Cf. NUC pre-56, v. 274, p. 256.
9	500	Signatures: [A]^2 B-K^4 L^2.
10	500	Printed on wove paper.
10	500	Press figures.
11	LN	Imperfect copy: leaf L2 (p. 75-[76]) lacking.
	655 7	Chronicles. $2 rbgenr
	755	Wove papers (Paper) $z France $y 18th century. $2 rbpap
	755	Press figures (Printing) $2 rbpri

PRINCIPAL *DCRB* RULES ILLUSTRATED

ref. no.

1	1A2, par. 3	(epigram omitted without using mark of omission)
2	4B1	(place of publication transcribed as it appears)
3	4C1	(publisher statement includes printer and booksellers)
4	4C2	(words or phrases preceding publisher statement transcribed; addresses omitted)
5	4C6, par. 1	(multiple publishers separated by prescribed punctuation)
6	4D6	(date uncertain; "one year or the other" pattern used)
7	5B3	(pagination sequence includes unnumbered pages)
8	7C6 (1)	(authorship note; source of attribution included)
9	7C9	(signatures note)
10	7C10	(physical description note)
11	7C18	(copy-specific note)

Presented in 1860.

Η ΚΑΙΝΗ

ΔΙΑΘΗΚΗ.

NOVUM

TESTAMENTUM.

JUXTA EXEMPLAR JOANNIS MILLII AC-
CURATISSIME IMPRESSUM.

Jas. S. Truscott

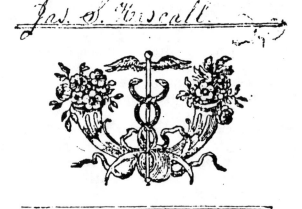

EDITIO PRIMA AMERICANA.

WIGORNIÆ, Massachusettensi:
Excudebat ISAIAS THOMAS, Jun.
Singulatim et numerose eo vendita officina sua.
Aprīl—1800.

EXAMPLE 46: Title page

EXAMPLE 46

CATALOG RECORD

ref. no.

	130 0	Bible. $p N. T. $l Greek. $s Mill. $f 1800.
3,4	245 13	[H¯e Kain¯e Diath¯ek¯e] = $b Novum Testamentum / $c juxta exemplar Joannis Millii accuratissime impressum.
5	250	Editio prima Americana.
1,2,3,6,7,8	260	Wigorniae [Worcester], Massachusettensi : $b Excudebat Isaias Thomas, Jun., sinoulatim [i.e. singulatim] et numerose eo vendita officina suae, $c April 1800.
9	300	478, [2] p. ; $c 18 cm. (12mo)
10	500	Greek text in double columns.
10	500	First three words in Greek characters on t.p.
11	500	Edited by Caleb Alexander. Cf. p. [3].
12	500	Signatures: A-2R⁶.
13	510 4	Evans $c 36952
14	500	Advertising matter on final leaf.
15	| LN	Bound in contemporary full leather, gilt-tooled spine and red leather spine label.
15	| LN	From the library of Jas. S. Hascall, with his signature.
	700 10	Mill, John, $d 1645-1707.
	700 10	Alexander, Caleb, $d 1755-1828, $e ed.
	700 10	Thomas, Isaiah, $c Jun., $d 1773-1819, $e printer.
	| LAE	Hascall, Jas. S., $e former owner.
16	740 01	Novum Testamentum.

PRINCIPAL *DCRB* RULES ILLUSTRATED

ref. no.

1	0G	(misprint transcribed as it appears)
2	0H, par. 2	(transcribe Latin ligature as component letters)
3	0H, par. 3	(convert to uppercase or lowercase according to AACR2; transcribe i/j and u/v according to pattern in main text)
4	1C	(title proper inclusive of parallel title)
5	2B1	(words or phrases associated with edition statement transcribed)
6	4B3	(modern form of place name added)
7	4C1	(publisher statement includes bookseller)
8	4D1	(month in date transcribed)
9	5D1, par. 3	(format)
10	7C2	(language of publication note)
11	7C6 (2)	(other statements of responsibility note)
12	7C9	(signatures note)
13	7C14	(references to published descriptions)
14	7C16	(informal contents note: advertisements)
15	7C18	(copy-specific note)
16	App. A.7C4-5	(added entry for parallel title)

Entered according to the act of congress, in the year 1832, by George
M'Dowell & George H. M'Dowell, in the clerk's office of the district court of
Maryland.

STEREOTYPED BY J. HOWE.

B.

GAZETTEER,

OR

GEOGRAPHICAL DICTIONARY,

OF

NORTH AMERICA AND THE WEST INDIES,

CONTAINING

I.—A GENERAL DESCRIPTION OF NORTH AMERICA. II.—A GENERAL DESCRIPTION OF
THE UNITED STATES; THE DECLARATION OF INDEPENDENCE AND CONSTITU
TION OF THE UNITED STATES. III.—A DESCRIPTION OF ALL THE STATES,
COUNTIES, CITIES, TOWNS, VILLAGES, FORTS, SEAS, HARBORS,
CAPES, RIVERS, LAKES, CANALS, RAIL-ROADS, MOUNTAINS, &c.

CONNECTED WITH NORTH AMERICA;

WITH THE EXTENT, BOUNDARIES AND NATURAL PRODUCTIONS OF EACH STATE; THE BEARING AND DISTANCE
OF REMARKABLE PLACES FROM EACH OTHER AND OF EACH FROM THE CITY OF WASHINGTON,
WITH THE POPULATION ACCORDING TO THE CENSUS OF 1830.

CONTAINING

LIKEWISE MANY TABLES RELATING TO THE COMMERCE, POPULATION, REVENUE,
DEBT, AND VARIOUS INSTITUTIONS OF THE UNITED STATES.

COMPILED FROM THE MOST RECENT AND AUTHENTIC SOURCES

BY BISHOP DAVENPORT.

Baltimore:
PUBLISHED BY GEORGE M'DOWELL & SON.

1833.

A.

EXAMPLE 47: A. Title page **B.** Title page verso

EXAMPLE 47

CATALOG RECORD

ref. no.

	100 1	Davenport, Bishop.
1	245 12	A new gazetteer, or geographical dictionary, of North America and the West Indies ... : $b compiled from the most recent and authentic sources / $c by Bishop Davenport.
2	260	Baltimore : $b Published by George M'Dowell & Son, $c 1833.
3,4,5	300	471, [1] p. (last p. blank), [2] folded leaves of plates : $b ill., maps ; $c 23 cm. (8vo)
6	500	"Stereotyped by J. Howe"--t.p. verso.
6	500	A variant of the edition described by Checklist Amer. imprints, with "sources" spelt correctly on t.p.
7	500	Copyright entered 1832 (t.p. verso).
8	500	Signatures: [A]^4 B-U^4 V^4 W^4 X-Z^4, 2A-2U^4 2V^4 2W^4 2X-2Z^4, 3A-3I^4.
9	500	Hand-colored maps of North America and the United States engraved by Young & Delleker.
9	500	Some wood engravings by R.S. Gilbert; one possibly cut by William Mason.
10	510 4	Checklist Amer. imprints, $c 18500
10	510 4	Thomson, T.R. Railroads, $c 719
10	510 4	Hamilton, S. Amer. book illustrators (1968 ed.), $c 1021
11	505 0	(from t.p.) I. A general description of North America -- II. A general description of the United States; the Declaration of Independence and Constitution of the United States -- III. A description of all the states, counties, cities, towns, villages, forts, seas, harbors, capes, rivers, lakes, canals, rail-roads, mountains, &c. connected with North America ...
12	LN	Library Company's copy imperfect: "A new" is cut from the top of the title page; inscribed: Joseph Thorne.
	655 7	Gazetteers. $2 rbgenr
	655 7	Maps $z North America. $2 rbgenr
	700 10	Gilbert, Reuben S., $e wood-engraver.
	700 10	Mason, William, $d fl. 1808-1844, $e wood-engraver.
	700 10	Young & Delleker, $e engraver.
	700 10	Howe, Jonathan, $e stereotyper.
	LAE	Thorne, Joseph, $e former owner.
	710 20	George M'Dowell & Son, $e publisher.
13	LTE	Gazetteer, or geographical dictionary, of North America and the West Indies ...

PRINCIPAL *DCRB* RULES ILLUSTRATED

ref. no.

1	1D2, par. 2	(other title information constitutes formal statement of contents)
2	4C2	(words or phrases preceding publisher statement transcribed)
3	5B3	(pagination sequence includes unnumbered pages)
4	5B7, par. 1	(expansion of statement of extent)
5	5D1, par. 3	(format)
6	7C7	(edition and bibliographic history note)
7	7C8	(publication note)
8	7C9	(signatures note)
9	7C10	(physical description note)
10	7C14	(references to published descriptions)
11	7C16	(formal contents (from t.p.) note)
12	7C18	(copy-specific note)
13	App. A.7C18	(added entry for copy-specific title)

C.

LETTRE

D'UN PAYSAN DE LA VALLÉE-NOIRE.

FANCHETTE.

ISIDORA

PAR

George Sand.

1

PARIS,
HIPPOLYTE SOUVERAIN, ÉDITEUR
De MM. George Sand, Frédéric Soulié, de Balzac, Alexandre Dumas, Paul de Kock,
Alphonse Brot, Amédée de Bast, Jules Lecomte, etc.
RUE DES BEAUX-ARTS, 5.
—
1846.

B.

A.

EXAMPLE 48: A. Title page to vol. 1 **B-C.** Section titles of works not listed on title page
(images reduced 25 percent)

EXAMPLE 48

CATALOG RECORD

ref. no.

	100 1	Sand, George, $d 1804-1876.
1	245 10	Isidora / $c par George Sand.
	260	Paris : $b Hippolyte Souverain ..., $c 1846.
2	300	3 v. (314, [2]; 309, [3]; 307 [i.e. 297], [3] p.) ; $c 21 cm.
3	500	First authorised edition; first published in 1845. Cf. Colin.
4	500	Pagination error in v. 3: p. 232 is followed by [3] p., pagination resumes with no. 246.
6	500	Vol. 3 also includes the author's Fanchette (p. [87]-232) and Lettre d'un paysan de la Vall´ee-Noir (p. [233]-307).
5	510 4	Colin, G. George Sand, $c p. 70-72.
5	510 4	Vicaire, G. Livres du 19. s., $c VII, 227-228
7	| LN	Copy 1 with the inkstamp of the Biblioth`eque de Tsarskoe Selo.
7	| LN	Copy 2 from the library of George Sand.
7	| LN	Copy 1 bound in green half sheep and marbled boards, edges sprinkled.
7	| LN	Copy 2 bound in two vols., uniformly with other author's copies in purple half morocco and marbled boards, edges marbled; spines numbered as vols. 41-42 of Sand's copies of her works; bookplate of H. Grandjean.
	700 12	Sand, George, $d 1804-1876. $t Fanchette. $f 1846.
	700 12	Sand, George, $d 1804-1876. $t Lettre d'un paysan de la Vall´ee-Noir. $f 1846.
	| LAE	Sand, George, $d 1804-1876, $e former owner.
8	740 01	Fanchette.
8	740 01	Lettre d'un paysan de la Vall´ee-Noir.
	| 755	Authors' copies (Provenance) $z France $y 19th century $2 rbprov

PRINCIPAL *DCRB* RULES ILLUSTRATED

ref. no.

1	1E2	(additional works not listed on title page)
2	5B20	(**option**: pagination of individual volumes given in parentheses after number of units)
3	7C7	(edition and bibliographic history note)
4	7C10	(physical description note)
5	7C14	(references to published descriptions)
6	7C16	(informal contents note)
7	7C18	(copy-specific note)
8	App. A.1E1-2	(added entry for title of additional work)

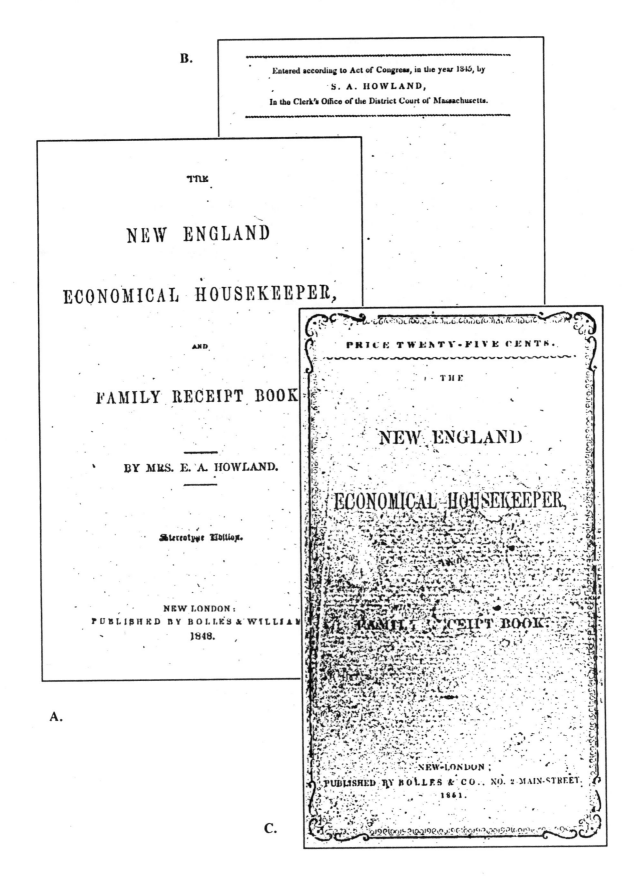

B.

Entered according to Act of Congress, in the year 1845, by
S. A. HOWLAND,
In the Clerk's Office of the District Court of Massachusetts.

THE

NEW ENGLAND

ECONOMICAL HOUSEKEEPER,

AND

FAMILY RECEIPT BOOK.

BY MRS. E. A. HOWLAND.

Stereotype Edition.

NEW LONDON:
PUBLISHED BY BOLLES & WILLIAM
1848.

A.

PRICE TWENTY-FIVE CENTS.

THE

NEW ENGLAND

ECONOMICAL HOUSEKEEPER,

AND

FAMILY RECEIPT BOOK.

NEW-LONDON:
PUBLISHED BY BOLLES & CO., NO. 2 MAIN-STREET.
1851.

C.

EXAMPLE 49: A. Title page B. Title page verso, showing copyright date C. Front cover,
showing date of impression (images reduced 20 percent)

EXAMPLE 49

CATALOG RECORD

ref. no.

	100 1		Howland, E. A. $q (Esther Allen), $d 1801-1860.
	245 14		The New England economical housekeeper and family receipt book / $c by Mrs. E.A. Howland.
	250		Stereotype edition.
1,2	260		New London [Conn.] : $b Published by Bolles & Williams, $c 1848, c1845 (1851 impression)
3	300		[6], 11-108 p. : $b ill. ; $c 18 cm.
4	500		First published 1844. Cf. Bitting, Kelly & Wheaton cited below.
5	500		Cover-title imprint dated 1851.
6	510 4		Bitting, K.G. Gastronomic bib., $c 236
6	510 4		Kelly & Wheaton. Bib. of culinary history, $c 3040-3050
7	500		Publisher's ads on lower board.
8	500		Includes index.
9		LN	Newspaper recipes pasted in at front, and on first blank at end.
9		LN	With the bookplate of Mrs. John T. Gernon.

PRINCIPAL *DCRB* RULES ILLUSTRATED

ref. no.

1	4C2	(words or phrases preceding publisher statement transcribed)
2	4E	(date of impression)
3	5B3	(pagination sequence includes unnumbered pages)
4	7C7	(edition and bibliographic history note)
5	7C8	(publication note)
6	7C14	(references to published descriptions)
7	7C16	(informal contents note; advertisements)
8	7C16	(informal contents note)
9	7C18	(copy-specific note)

CHARLES DE GAULLE

LE FIL
DE L'ÉPÉE

GRAVURES AU BURIN
LBERT DECARIS

JUSTIFICATION DU TIRAGE

Le tirage de cette édition a été limité à 450 exemplaires sur vélin de Rives, dont : 5 exemplaires, numérotés de 1 à 5, auxquels on a ajouté une double-planche gravée et encrée, un dessin original double-page, une gravure refusée, une suite sur Auvergne et une suite sur soie de toutes les gravures; 15 exemplaires, numérotés de 6 à 20, auxquels on a ajouté une planche gravée et encrée, un dessin original, une gravure refusée, une suite sur Auvergne de toutes les gravures et le tirage sur soie du frontispice et des cinq planches doubles; 55 exemplaires, numérotés de 21 à 75, auxquels on a ajouté une gravure refusée, une suite sur Auvergne de toutes les gravures et le tirage sur soie du frontispice; 375 exemplaires, numérotés de 76 à 450. Il a été imprimé en outre 25 exemplaires hors-commerce, qui ont été justifiés de I à XXV.

EXEMPLAIRE N° 448

ACHEVÉ D'IMPRIMER LE CINQ DÉCEMBRE MIL NEUF CENT SOIXANTE-TROIS PAR DOMINIQUE VIGLINO POUR LE TEXTE ET PAR JACQUES RIGAL POUR LES GRAVURES.

LUBINEAU, ÉDITEUR
A PARIS

EXAMPLE 50: A. Title page B. Page [4], showing limitation statement C. Colophon
(images reduced 35 percent)

EXAMPLE 50

CATALOG RECORD

ref. no.

	100 1	Gaulle, Charles de, $d 1890-1970.
1	245 13	Le fil de l'´ep´ee / $c Charles de Gaulle ; gravures au burin d'Albert Decaris.
2,3,4	260	A Paris : $b Marcel Lubineau, ´editeur, $c [5 Dec. 1963]
5,6	300	188, [8] p. : $b ill. ; $c 35 cm. (fol.)
7	500	Author's name transposed from head of title.
8	500	"Le tirage de cette ´edition a ´et´e limit´e `a 450 exemplaires sur v´elin de Rives ... Il a ´et´e imprim´e en outre 25 exemplaires hors-commerce, qui ont ´et´e justifi´es de I `a XXV"--p. [4].
11	LN	Library has copy no. 448.
9	500	Date of publication from colophon: Achev´e d'imprimer le cinq d´ecembre mil neuf cent soixante-trois par Dominique Viglino pour le texte et par Jacques Rigal pour les gravures.
10	500	In loose quires, issued in a portfolio within a protective case.
	700 10	Decaris, Albert.
	655 7	Livres d'artistes. $2 rbgenr
	755	Limitation statements (Publishing) $2 rbpub

PRINCIPAL *DCRB* RULES ILLUSTRATED

ref. no.

1	1G3	(statement of responsibility transposed without using mark of omission)
2	4B2	(words or phrases associated with place name transcribed)
3	4D1	(day and month in date transcribed)
4	4D2, par. 3	(very long verbal date statement transcribed as formalized date)
5	5B3	(pagination sequence includes unnumbered pages)
6	5D1, par. 3	(format)
7	7C6 (4)	(statement of responsibility note: name transposed)
8	7C7	(edition and bibliographic history note)
9	7C8	(publication note)
10	7C10	(physical description note)
11	7C18	(copy-specific note)

RULE INDEX

GENERAL RULES

TITLE AND STATEMENT OF RESPONSIBILITY AREA

PHYSICAL DESCRIPTION AREA

APPENDICES

TITLE INDEX

TITLE INDEX

NAME INDEX

TOPICAL INDEX

Note: Terms in parentheses refer to rules and to paragraph numbers within rules.

A

Abbreviations
>Tironian sign, expansion of (0J2), ex. 3, 5-6
>*see also* Contraction, marks of, expansion; Initials.

Academic degrees, honors, etc.
>omitted from statement of responsibility (1G8), ex. 16, 24-25, 28-29
>retained in statement of responsibility (1G8), ex. 19, 21, 30, 32-33

Accents (0H.1), ex. 13, 19, 29, 32-34, 42

Acronyms, *see* Initials

Added entries
>for alternative title (App. A.1B3), ex. 14, 23, 26A-27, 29, 34, 38, 40A, 40C
>for chief title (App. A.1B1), ex. 3, 7-8, 11-12, 14, 20-21, 25, 28, 30
>for copy-specific binder's title (App. A.7C18), ex. 26A-26B, 35
>for copy-specific title (App. A.7C18), ex. 47
>for other title (App. A.7C4-5), ex. 11, 27
>for parallel title (App. A.7C4-5), ex. 28, 46
>for title of additional work (App. A.1E1-2), ex. 12, 23, 30, 38, 42, 48
>for title proper (App. A.1B1), ex. 36
>>in modern orthography (App. A.0H), ex. 7, 20, 23, 27
>>with expansion of contractions (App. A.0J2), ex. 3, 6, 12, 21
>>without expansion of contractions (App. A.0J2), ex. 6
>for title variant (App. A7C4-7C5), ex. 7, 16-17, 20

Additional titles, *see* Other title information, additional titles

Address of printer as substitute for name in source (4C4), ex. 8

Address of publisher, etc.
>option to include in publisher statement (4C2), ex. 8, 28, 37

Advertisements in informal contents note (7C16), ex. 31, 43, 46, 49

æ (Latin ligature) transcribed as "ae" (0H), ex. 8, 12, 16, 23, 25, 28, 30, 46

Alternative titles
>added entries for (App. A.1B3), ex. 14, 23, 26A-27, 29, 34, 38, 40A, 40C
>included in title proper (1B3), ex. 14, 23, 27, 29, 34, 38, 40A-40C

"Anno," and similar words, used with date of publication, etc. (4D1), ex. 3, 4, 6-7, 9-10, 17, 19-20, 25, 32

Appendices, subsidiary texts, etc. (1G14, 2C3, App. A), ex. 12, 19, 23, 25, 30, 35, 38, 42, 48

Arabic numerals
>added to transcribed form of date when not arabic (4D2.1), ex. 13
>and roman numerals in same sequence of pagination (5B6), ex. 30, 39, 42
>substituted for chronograms in date of publication, etc. (4D2.2), ex. 23
>substituted for roman numerals in date of publication, etc. (4D2.1), ex. 2-3, 6-7, 11, 14, 16-17, 22, 31, 33, 35-36, 38, 40A-40C, 43

Author statement, *see* Statements of responsibility; Statements of responsibility relating to edition

Authorship, notes relating to (7C6.1), ex. 2, 16, 23, 27, 34, 39, 43-45

Autographs (7C18), ex. 5, 9, 22, 31, 33, 35, 46, 47

Avant-titre, *see* Other title information

TOPICAL INDEX

F

Fictitious attribution to a person (7C6), ex. 16, 23, 34,
Fictitious publication, etc., details (4A4, 4C5), ex. 15, 39
Folded leaves (5B10), ex. 30, 47
Foliation (by count of leaves), *see* Extent, statement of; Pagination
Foliation (by signature) (7C9), ex. 2-6, 7-10, 12-14, 16-17, 19-25, 26A-26B, 30-31, 33, 39-40A, 42-43, 45-47
Format (5D1), ex. 2-8, 10-12, 14-16, 19-21, 23-26B, 28-44, 46-47, 50
French folds (as separate publications), *see* Single-sheet publications

G

Gaskell's formula (signatures) (7C9), ex. 2-10, 12-17, 19-26B, 30-31, 33, 39-40A, 42-43, 45-47
Gothic capitals, transcription of (0H.5), ex. 3-4, 6, 17
Graphic process or technique, option to add to illustration statement (5C1), ex. 4, 23, 30, 34
Gregorian calendar and date(s) of publication, etc. (4D2.5), ex. 2, 4
Guide letters (0G), ex. 2

H

Headings given in "with" notes (7C19), ex. 3-4
Headpieces not regarded as illustrations (5C1), ex. 13-14, 23, 29, 31, 33-34, 38, 40A
Height (of volume), *see* Size
Holdings, library's, *see* Library's holdings
Honor, titles of, in statement of responsibility (1G7), ex. 3-4, 19, 29, 31, 34, 37
Hyphen, use of, in title proper of multivolumed works (1B4), ex. 11

I

i (letter) transcribed as j (App. B), ex. 3-4, 6-7, 12, 14, 17, 23
I (letter) transcribed for "ii" (0H, App. B), ex. 21
"i.e.", use of
        with corrections to misprints (0G, App. A), ex. 23, 46
        with corrections to publication information (4A4, 4B5, 4B9, 4C5, 4D2, 4E), ex. 9, 11, 34, 46
        with corrections to statement of extent (5B7), ex. 24, 26A-26B, 48
Illustrated title page
        not regarded as illustration (5C1), ex. 23
        not treated as a plate (5B9), ex. 23
Illustration statement (5C), ex. 4, 17, 23, 25, 27, 30, 32, 36, 40A-40C, 44, 47, 49-50
        option to add graphic process or technique (5C1), ex. 4, 23, 30, 34
Illustrations
        illustrated title pages not regarded as (5C1), ex. 23
        numbering (5C4), ex. 27

M

on statements of responsibility (1G2-1G3, 7C6), ex. 2, 16, 23-24, 27, 33-34, 36, 39, 43-46, 50

on statements of responsibility transposed to precede edition statement (2C2), ex. 33

on supplied place of publication (4B10, 4B12), ex. 1, 5, 22-23, 41

on title proper (0C3, 1B1, 1B4-1B5, 7C3), ex. 1-2, 11, 18, 41, 44

on translations (7C2), ex. 11, 13, 19, 25, 36, 42

on transposition of data (1B1, 1G3, 2C2, 7C6, 7C7), ex. 17, 33, 36, 50

on true attribution to a person in presence of incorrect data (7C6), ex. 16, 23, 34

on variant publisher statements in multipart or multivolume items (4C7, 4D8, 7C8), ex. 29

on variations in title (1B4, 7C4), ex. 7, 11, 16, 20, 27

on volumes as bound (5B16), ex. 29, 34

option to add to minimal-level records (App. D), ex. 40C

"with" notes (7C19), ex. 3-4, 44

Marks of contraction, expansion of (0J2, 7C9, App. A), ex. 3, 5-9, 12, 21

Marks of omission, *see* Omission, marks of

Minimal-level records (DCRB) (App. D), ex. 40B-40C

Misprints, etc., *see* Errors in item

Monograph title page as source of series information (0D), ex. 43

Mottoes on title page, omission of (1A2), ex. 39

Multipart items

extent (5B16-5B17, 5B20), ex. 1, 11, 18, 29, 32, 34-35, 38, 44, 48

use of contents note (7C16), ex. 35, 48

with changes in publisher, etc. (4C7), ex. 29

with continuous pagination (5B19), ex. 32

with title proper including numbering, etc. (1B4), ex. 11

with two or more dates of publication, etc. (4D8), ex. 11, 18

without continuous pagination, option to record pagination of each unit (5B20), ex. 11, 48

Multivolume items, *see* Multipart items

N

Nobility, titles of, in statement of responsibility (1G7), ex. 22, 35

Non-Christian-era date(s), *see* Calenders and date(s) of publication, etc.

Notes

bibliographic citations in (7C6, 7C14), ex. 1-5, 8-9, 12, 14-17, 22-24, 26A-26B, 30, 32, 34, 36-37, 39, 41, 43-44, 46-49

copy-specific (0G, 7C7, 7C18), ex. 1-14, 16-17, 19-26, 29, 31-39, 41-50
see also Copy-specific notes

giving full collation (7C9), ex. 15

in a work, phrases about on title page (1G14.2, 2C3, App. A.1G14), ex. 1, 3, 19, 24-25

mandatory, *see* Mandatory notes

on additional imprint information (4A2), ex. 1-6, 9

on additional titles not named on t.p. (1E2), ex. 48

on advertisements (5B5), ex. 31, 43, 46, 49

on authorship (7C6.1), ex. 2, 16, 23, 27, 34, 39, 43-45

on bibliographical description of work based on imperfect copy (0B2, 5B12, 7C18), ex. 19

TOPICAL INDEX

O

TOPICAL INDEX

P

TOPICAL INDEX

Q

Qualifications, academic
    omitted from statement of responsibility (1G8), ex. 16, 25, 29
    retained in statement of responsibility (1G8), ex. 28, 30
Question mark, use of
    with supplied publisher where uncertain (4C8), ex. 1
    with uncertain date(s) of publication, etc. (4D5-4D6), ex. 5
    with uncertain place of publication (4B12), ex. 1

R

"References" notes (7C7, 7C14), ex. 1-5, 8-9, 12, 14-17, 22-24, 26A-26B, 30, 32, 34, 36-37, 39, 41, 43-44, 46-49
Reimpression, *see* Impression
Roman dates, *see* Calenders and date(s) of publication, etc.
Roman numerals
    capitalization (0H, 5B1), ex. 30
    changed to arabic numerals in date of publication (4D2.1), ex. 2-3, 6-7, 9, 11, 14, 16-17, 22, 31, 33, 35-36, 38, 40A-40C, 43
    erroneous or misprinted in date(s) of publication, etc. (4D2.4), ex. 9
    option to transcribe as they appear in date(s) of publication, etc. (4D2.1), ex. 13
    pagination (5B1), ex. 8, 30
Romanization, use of for title proper (7C4), ex. 2, 10, 46
Rubrication (7C18), ex. 1
Running title, added entries for (App. A), ex. 7, 16, 20

S

s (letter), transcribed in modern form (App. B), ex. 3-9, 11, 13-17, 19-20, 23-32, 34, 36-38, 40A-40C, 42-43
"s.n.", use of (4C9), ex. 5, 23, 41
Sections of items, punctuation between
    preceding each unit of other title information, ex. 15, 26A-26B, 35, 42
    preceding each subsequent statement of responsibility (1A1), ex. 15, 26A-26B, 35, 42
    with titles of parts by same person(s) or body (bodies) (1E1), ex. 12
Sheets, *see* Single-sheet publications
"sic", use of (0G), ex. 23
Sign, Tironian, treated as abbreviation (0J2), ex. 3, 5-6
Signatures (gatherings) (7C9), ex. 2-10, 12-17, 19-26B, 30-31, 33, 39-40A, 42-43, 45-47
    signed with unavailable characters (7C9), ex. 2, 6, 16, 19, 25
Sine nomine (s.n.) (4C9), ex. 5, 23, 41
Single-sheet publications (1F)
    extent (5B2, 5B15-5B16), ex. 41, 27
    normally imposed single sheets (5B2), ex. 41
    prescribed source of information (0D), ex. 27
    size (5D5), ex. 27

TOPICAL INDEX

TOPICAL INDEX

Transposition of data
　　edition statement and statement of responsibility (2C2), ex. 33
　　generally not indicated by marks of omission (1A2), ex. 6-7, 16, 29, 31, 33-34, 36-37, 39, 40A-40C, 42, 45
　　noting original position of elements and/or areas on t.p. (1B1, 1G3, 2C2-2C3, 7C6-7C7), ex. 17, 33, 36, 50
　　title proper and other titles or other title information (1B3), ex. 14, 23, 27, 29, 34, 38, 40A-40C
　　title proper and statement of responsibility (1G3), ex. 36, 50

U

u (letter), transcribed as v (0H, App. A-B), ex. 4, 15, 17
Uniform titles, option to transcribe in "with" note (7C19), ex. 3-4
Unnumbered pages or leaves
　　in foliation sequence (5B3), ex. 3, 6, 9-11, 13, 15, 17
　　in pagination sequence (5B3), ex. 2, 4-5, 7, 12, 16, 19-26, 30-33, 37, 39-43, 45-50

V

v (letter), transcribed as u (0H), ex. 3, 5-9, 11, 13, 15-16, 19, 23
Vignettes not regarded as illustrations (5C1), ex. 11, 13, 15-21, 28, 30
Virgule, transcription of when used as comma (0E), ex. 17
Volumes, number of (1A2, 1D3, 5B16-5B17, 5B20)
　　issued and bound in different number of volumes (5B16.3), ex. 29, 34
　　pagination (5B20), ex. 11, 32, 48
　　publication of in more than one physical unit (5B16), ex. 1, 11, 18, 29, 32, 34-35, 38, 44, 48
　　statement of omitted (1A2.3-4), ex. 34-35, 48
　　transcribed as other title information (1D3), ex. 35-36, 38, 40A-40C
　　transcribed as part of title proper (1B4), ex. 11

W

w (letter), transcribed as vv (0H), ex. 20
Width (of volume), *see* Size
"With" notes (7C19), ex. 3-4, 44
Woodcuts
　　as part of extent (5C1), ex. 4
　　in physical description note (7C10), ex. 5, 17, 32
Words or phrases
　　as supplied title (1B5, 1E2), ex. 2, 18, 48
　　explanatory
　　　　with edition statement (2B1), ex. 12, 19, 21, 24-25, 30, 33, 43, 46
　　　　with place of publication (4B2), ex. 2-4, 9-11, 13, 15, 17, 19-20, 29, 32-34, 42, 50

with publisher statement (4C6), ex. 7, 19-20, 24, 27, 29, 30-31, 35, 45
in single-sheet publications (1F2), ex. 27
omitted without using marks of omission (1A2.3-4)
       bible verse, ex. 16, 40A-40C
       epigram, ex. 29, 31, 36-37, 42, 45
       motto, ex. 39
       privilege statement, ex. 6-7, 29, 33
       volume statement, ex. 34, 35, 48
on t.p. notes, appendices, etc., in work (1G14), ex. 17, 22, 24, 36, 42
option to devise title for collection without meaningful title (1E2), ex. 18
option to transcribe as they appear in date of publication (4D1), ex. 2-4, 6-7, 9-10, 15, 17, 19-20, 25, 32, 46, 50
with name of principal place of publication (4B2), ex. 2-4, 9-11, 13, 15, 17, 19-20, 29, 32-34, 42, 50
with statements of responsibility (1G7-1G8), ex. 3-4, 16, 19, 24-25, 28-29, 31-33, 34, 37